HISTORY IN THE MAKING
Series Editor: J. A. P. Jones

2 The Medieval World

HISTORY IN THE MAKING

J. A. P. Jones

Headmaster
Poynton County High School
Cheshire

2 The Medieval World

M

Macmillan Education
London and Basingstoke

First published 1979
Reprinted 1980, 1981, 1982, 1983

Published by
MACMILLAN EDUCATION LIMITED
Houndmills Basingstoke Hampshire RG21 2XS
and London
Associated companies in Delhi Dublin
Hong Kong Johannesburg Lagos Melbourne
New York Singapore and Tokyo

Filmset in Great Britain by
Cox & Wyman Ltd, London, Fakenham and Reading
Printed in Hong Kong

For Christopher

Series preface

Changes in the teaching of History over the last decade have raised many problems, to which there are no easy solutions. The classification of objectives, the presentation of material in varied and appropriate language, the use and abuse of evidence and the reconsideration of assessment techniques are four of the more important. Many teachers are now encouraging their pupils individually or in groups to participate in the processes and skills of the professional historian. Moreover such developments are being discussed increasingly in the context of mixed ability classes and the need to provide suitable teaching approaches for them.

History in the Making is a new course for secondary schools intended for pupils of average ability. It is a contribution to the current debate, and provides one possible way forward. It accepts many of the proven virtues of traditional courses: the fascination of the good tale, the drama of human life, individual and collective, the need to provide a visual stimulus to support the written word.

But it has built on to these some of the key features of the 'new history' so that teachers can explore, within the framework of a text book, many of the 'new' approaches and techniques. To this end each chapter in this volume has four major components.

1 **The text** This provides the basic framework of the chapters, and although the approach is essentially factual, it is intended to arouse and sustain the interest of the reader of average ability.

2 **The illustrations** These have been carefully selected to stand beside the written pieces of evidence in the chapter, and to provide (so far as is possible) an authentic visual image of the period/topic. Photographs, artwork and maps are all used to clarify and support the text, and to develop the pupil's powers of observation.

3 **Using the evidence** This is a detailed study of the evidence on one particular aspect of the chapter. Did the Walls of Jericho really come tumbling down? Was the death of William Rufus in the New Forest really an accident? What was the background to the torpedoing of the *Lusitania*? These are the sort of questions which are asked, to give the pupil the opportunity to consider not only the problems facing the historian, but also those facing the characters of history. Different forms of documentary evidence are considered, as well as archaeological, architectural, statistical, and other kinds of source material; the intention is to give the pupil a genuine, if modest, insight into the making of history.

4 **Questions and further work** These are intended to test and develop the pupil's reading of the chapter, and in particular the *Using the evidence* section. Particular attention is paid to the development of historical skills, through the examination and interpretation of evidence. The differences between primary and secondary sources, for example, are explored, and concepts such as bias in evidence introduced through specific examples. Some comprehension questions are included, but the emphasis is very much on involving

5

pupils with the materials, and helping them to develop a critical awareness of different kinds of evidence and its limitations. By applying the skills which they have developed, pupils may then be able to formulate at a suitable level and in appropriate language, ideas and hypotheses of their own.

History in the Making is a complete course in five volumes, to meet the needs of pupils between the ages of 11–16 (in other words up to and including the first public examination). However each volume stands by itself and may be used independently of the others; given the variety of syllabuses in use in schools today this flexibility is likely to be welcomed by many teachers. *The Ancient World* and *The Medieval World* are intended primarily for 11–13-year-old pupils, *The Early Modern World*, for 12–14-year-old pupils, *Britain, Europe and beyond, 1700–1900* for pre-CSE pupils and *The Twentieth Century* for CSE examination candidates.

It is our hope that pupils will be encouraged, within the main topics and themes of British, European and World History, to experience for themselves the stimulus and challenge, the pleasure and frustration, the vitality and humanity that are an essential part of History in the Making.

J. A. P. Jones

Contents

Introduction   10

The making of Christian Europe

1 **The barbarian invasions**   14
   Using the evidence: the Sutton Hoo ship burial
2 **Europe becomes Christian**   26
   Using the evidence: Bede and the meeting at Whitby (664)
3 **The Mediterranean world**   36
   Using the evidence: the Battle of Poitiers (732)
4 **Charlemagne**   46
   Using the evidence: the conversion of the Saxons
5 **The Vikings**   58
   Using the evidence: the Vikings and Vinland

The powers of Europe

6   **The Normans**   74
    Using the evidence: the Battle of Hastings
7   **The two archbishops**   86
    Using the evidence: Thomas Becket
8   **The king's government**   96
    Using the evidence: the death of William Rufus
9   **The Crusades**   106
    Using the evidence: the Siege of Acre (1190)
10 **The power of the towns**   120
    Using the evidence: English overseas trade

Medieval life

11 **Life on the manor**   134
    Using the evidence: the Church and village life
12 **Life in the towns**   146
    Using the evidence: the Chester Cycle of plays
13 **The aristocracy and chivalry**   160
    Using the evidence: becoming a knight
14 **Monks and friars**   170
    Using the evidence: the White Monks
15 **Life at school and university**   180
    Using the evidence: medical teaching

The later Middle Ages

16 **Kings and people**   190
    Using the evidence: why was there a Peasants' Revolt?
17 **The Hundred Years War**   202
    Using the evidence: Joan of Arc
18 **The later medieval Church**   214
    Using the evidence: the Lollards

Acknowledgements

The author and publishers wish to thank the following who have kindly given permission for the use of copyright material:

Associated Book Publishers Limited for extracts from *England under the Normans and Angevins* by H. W. C. Davis, published by Methuen and Co. Ltd; *English Historical Documents*, Volume IV 1327–1485 edited by Alec R. Myers, published by Eyre & Spottiswoode (Publishers) Ltd; *William the Conqueror* (English Monarchs Series) by D. C. Douglas, published by Eyre & Spottiswoode (Publishers) Ltd, and *English Historical Documents*, Volume II 1042–1189 edited by D. C. Douglas & G. W. Greenway, published by Eyre & Spottiswoode (Publishers) Ltd;

J. J. Bagley for an extract from *Historical Interpretation*, Volume I;

B. T. Batsford Limited for an extract from *Everyday Life in Medieval Times* edited by Marjorie Rowling;

Cambridge University Press for extracts from *Medieval Lincoln* by J. W. F. Hill and *Life in the Middle Ages* by C. G. Coulton;

Cassell Limited for an extract from *History of the English Speaking Peoples* by Sir Winston Churchill;

Hutchinson Publishing Group Limited for an extract from *Portraits and Documents*, Volume 3 by D. Baker;

John Johnson on behalf of the Estate of Henry Treece for an extract from *Know about the Crusades* by Henry Treece;

Longman Group Limited for extracts from *Medieval History of Europe* by R. H. C. Davis; *Alfred and the Danes* and *The Medieval Monastery* (Then and There Series) by M. Reeves and *The Vikings* (Then and There Series) by G. L. Proctor;

Macdonald and Jane's Publishers Ltd for an extract from *Joan of Arc* by Regine Pernoud;

Oxford University Press for extracts from *Alfred of Rievaulx* edited by M. Powicke, *Gesta Francorum* edited by Rosalind Hill and *Monastic Constitutions of Lanfranc* edited by Dom David Knowles from *Oxford Medieval Texts Series* and *The Paston Letters* edited by N. Davis (1971) and *From Domesday Book to Magna Carta 1087–1216* by A. L. Poole (2nd edition 1955);

Penguin Books Limited for extracts from *Two Lives of Charlemagne* by Einhard and Notker, translated by Lewis Thorpe, Penguin Classics 1969, pp 76–7, 79, 71, 84, 61, 63 and 153 © translation Lewis Thorpe 1969, and extracts from *Chronicles of the Crusades* translated by M. R. B. Shaw, Penguin Classics 1963, © translation M. R. B. Shaw 1963.

The author and publisher wish to acknowledge the following photograph sources:

Reproduced by Gracious Permission of Her Majesty The Queen p. 193 left; Aerofilms pp. 15, 22 top, 60 top, 77, 112, 119; Archiv fur Kunst und Geschichte p. 210 right; Archives Photographiques, Paris title page, p. 73; Ashmolean Museum (Dept of Antiquities) p. 65; Barnabys Picture Library p. 94; Bayer Staatsbibliothek, Munchen p. 129; Belgium National Tourist Office p. 127; Bib. Nationale, Paris pp. 96, 97, 115, 205; Bildarchiv Foto, Marburg p. 48; Bodleian Library pp. 20 (Ms Douce. 178, f. 406ʳ) 21 bottom (Ms Douce. 178, f. 181ᵛ) 99 bottom right (Ms Canon. Misc. 476, f. 79ᵛ) 130 (Ms Douce. 208, f. 120ᵛ) 138 Ms. Douce. 88, f. 51) 141 (Ms. Bodley 264, Roll. 93) 167 (Ms. Bodl. 264, f. 112) 169, 183 (Ms. New College, C288–P3562) 187 top (Ms. Univ. Coll. 165, p. 91) 197 top (Ms. Laud. Misc. 720, f. 225ʳ); British Library pp 46 (Cotton Ms. Domit, Axvii, f. 122ᵛ) 67 (Stowe Ms. 944, f. 6) 95 (Harley Ms. 5102, f. 32) 114 bottom (Add. Ms. 42130, f. 82) 120, 131 (Add. 42130, f. 173ᵛ) top (Royal Ms. 15E III, f. 269) 134 (Harley Ms. 4381, f. 34) 136/137 (Add. Ms. 42130, 170ᵛ) 139 top, 145 (Royal 2B VII, f. 82ᵛ) Add Ms. 24098, f. 266) 164 right, 166 (Harley 4379, f. 19ᵛ) (Lansdowne Ms. 158, f. 14) 178 (Harley Roll Y.6.) 181 left 200, 206 (Royal Ms. 17E. III, f. 36) (Royal Ms. 14E IV, f. 10) (Cotton Ms. julius E iv, f. 8ᵛ) 207 (Roy. Ms. 14. EIV f. 57) 213 (Cotton Ms. julius E iv, art 6, f. 18ᵛ) Trustees of the British Museum title page, pp. 13, 14, 19 top, 21 top, 24, 25, 66, 192, 200, 200/201; Bulloz pp. 53, 57, 150, 151, 164 left, 176 bottom, 208; Burgerbibliothek, Bern p. 116; Cambridge University Collection (J. K. St Joseph) pp. 142, 174; Camera Press pp. 10, 114 top, 163; Peter Clayton pp. 82 left, 101; Crown Copyright, Dept of Environment pp. 34, 170; Michael Dixon p. 69; Edinburgh University Library p. 39; Genshmigung Des Rosgartenmuseums, Konstanz p. 217 top; Giraudon pp. 51, 195, 210 left, 212, 214, 218; Sonia Halliday pp. 37, 109, 172/3

top; Hampshire County Council p. 22 bottom; His Grace The Archbishop of Canterbury and the Trustees of Lambeth Palace Library p. 209; Michael Holford pp. 75 right, 76, 84, 85; A. F. Kersting pp. 28, 52 bottom, 54, 161 bottom left, 190; Lincolnshire Library Service pp. 146, 149 left, 153 bottom; Mansell Collection pp. 36, 38, 82 right, 87, 88 right, 90, 100, 103 bottom, 105, 121, 122 top, 124, 147 right, 155, 156, 165, 172, 175, 176 top, 179, 181 right, 182 bottom, 185, 186, 188 bottom, 191 top left, 194, 215, 216, 217 bottom, 219 top, 221, 222; Masters of the Bench of the Inner Temple p. 98 bottom, 103 top, 113; Museen fur Kunst und Kulturgeschichte, Lubeck p. 122 bottom; Museum of London p. 219 bottom; Crown Copyright, National Records pp. 32 top right, 80 right, 81, 131 bottom, 135 left, 136 left, 147 left, 161 top right, 193 right; National Portrait Gallery pp. 191 top right, centre left, centre right, bottom; National Museum, Denmark p. 63; Oxford City Council p. 148; Pflichtvermerr Verbstenktung p.55 right; Picturepoint pp. 99 bottom left, 110, 125, 177; Popperfoto pp. 40/41 top, 182 top; Press Assoc. p. 11; Crown Copyright, Public Record Office pp. 79, 80 left, 98 top, 132, 153 top; Rijksmuseum, Amsterdam p. 126; Crown Copyright, Royal Commission Historical Monuments p. 161 bottom right; RTHPL pp. 18, 40/41 bottom, 99 top right, 173 bottom right, 180, 188 top, 197 bottom, 198; Crown Copyright, Science Museum pp. 58, 59; Ronald Sheridan pp. 43 top, 143, 211; Royal Library, Copenhagen p. 71; Walter Scott, Bradford p. 149 left; Snark International pp. 33, 88 left, 107, 144, 171, 173 bottom left, 204; Staatsbibliothek Bamberg p. 48; Stofmun Arni Magnussonar, Reykjavik p. 64; Eric Taylor p. 43 bottom right; Trinity College Library pp. 196, 201; Universitetets Oldsakamling, Oslo pp. 60 bottom, 72; University Library, Cambridge pp. 75 left, 139 bottom, 187 middle and bottom; Victoria & Albert Museum pp. 17, 43 bottom left, 161 top left; H. Roger Viollet pp. 44, 168; Terry Watson p. 23; Wayland Picture Library title page, pp. 133, 189; G. Wheeler p. 12; York Minster Library p. 30.

The publishers have made every effort to trace all the copyright holders, but if they have inadvertently overlooked any, they will be pleased to make the necessary arrangements at the first opportunity.

List of Maps

Invasions of the Roman Empire   16
The spread of Christianity in Britain   31
The empire of Justinian I   36
The world of Islam AD 732   41
Islamic Spain   42
The empire of Charlemagne   49
Viking raiders and settlers   62
Viking England   67
The North Atlantic   68
Saxon England   74
Norman England   78
The campaigns of 1066   83
Twelfth-century Europe   102
Crusading routes   110
The kingdom of Jerusalem   115
The Hanseatic League   121
Medieval trade routes   123
The wool trade   127
The Hundred Years War   202

Cover illustration courtesy of
Bibliothèque Nationale/Robert Harding Associates

Author's Acknowledgements

In preparing this volume I have benefited particularly from the
enthusiasm and interest of Peter Greenleaf and David Cogger, Heads of
History respectively at Huddersfield New College and Verdin Com-
prehensive School, Winsford. I have been taught much by the pupils at
both these schools: they have helped to give this book both purpose and
pleasure. Lastly I am grateful to Mrs Loretta Kemp who typed the
original manuscript.

Introduction

The Great Train Robbery

In the early hours of every morning, a train hurtles through the Buckinghamshire countryside and shatters the peace of the night. On board is the mail from Scotland for London.

But the night of 8 August 1964 was different. As the train approached the lonely Sears Crossing near Cheddington, a signal was down. The driver slowed the train: what was wrong? Was there an accident at the crossing? The train ground to a halt.

Suddenly at the driver's back were two men, dressed in boiler suits, their faces hidden by balaclava helmets. The guard in the mail van was attacked by other men similarly dressed. The guard and driver were bound and gagged, and the men escaped into the night with £2 517 975. This was the biggest robbery in British history.

Who were these train robbers? Detectives from London's Flying Squad, led by Detective Chief Superintendent Butler, were quickly on the scene. In order to solve the crime, they had to find evidence. First they interviewed the guard and driver, but they found out very little because the robbers had been masked.

Then they found a deserted farm, near to Sears Crossing. There they struck lucky. There were signs that it had been occupied a few days before. In the farmyard were a lorry and two Land-Rovers. Nearby they found the remains of a hastily-lit bonfire. Round it on the ground were charred fragments of mailbags and banknote wrappings.

The detectives went to work on the farm. They combed every centimetre of it. It had been washed down by the robbers but hurriedly and carelessly. Fingerprint men found prints on the lorry, the side of a cat's dish, in the bathroom, and on a bottle of tomato ketchup.

The farmhouse, near Sears Crossing

Examining the evidence at the farm

In London the prints were checked against those of known criminals. Eight men were identified. The hunt for them began. Two were discovered buying cars with five-pound notes. Some of these were definitely stolen from the train. The men were taken back to the house where they were staying and a further £155 000 was found.

A third man was caught with £131 in his possession. Again some of the notes came from the train. He had another £12 000 in his flat. He said a friend had won it gambling, but he could not produce this friend. In all seven men were arrested and brought to trial at Aylesbury in Buckinghamshire, charged with robbery while armed with offensive weapons.

The evidence against them was read out. The jury decided that beyond all reasonable doubt the seven were guilty of robbery. They were sentenced to thirty years' imprisonment.

Evidence is information. Like the detective, the historian has information which he uses to solve the mysteries of the past. Consider the following mystery where the historian can use the clues to solve the problem. In this case it too is a crime.

The Murder of the Princes in the Tower

In the year 1483 Edward IV, king of England, died quite suddenly. He left two sons, Edward and Richard, aged twelve and ten, to succeed him. Because they were so young the dead king's brother, Richard, Duke of Gloucester, was named as regent.

In early summer, the two princes were observed playing in the gardens of the Tower of London. In June they were seen behind barred windows in the Tower. But they were never seen or heard of again. In July, Richard of Gloucester became king as Richard III.

What happened to the two boys? We have some evidence to help us. In looking for it, the historian is being a detective. First he may interview Polydore Vergil, a chronicler writing twenty years after King Edward's death:

(1) King Richard, after his coronation, lived in continual fear and therefore determined to kill his nephews because they were a danger to him. Therefore he sent an order to Robert Brackenbury, the lieutenant of the Tower of London, to murder them quickly by some convenient method.... But this lieutenant was astonished at the cruelty of this and refused.... The king therefore gave the order to another, James Tyrrel, who rode sorrowfully to London and murdered those royal children. But with what kind of death they were executed is not certainly known.

Then the historian can interview a second chronicler, 'Thomas More', who wrote about the same time:

(2) In 1502 when Sir James Tyrrel and John Dighton were in prison for treason, they made a confession that they murdered the two young princes. This was their confession.

When King Richard was on his way to Gloucester in August 1483 he sent one

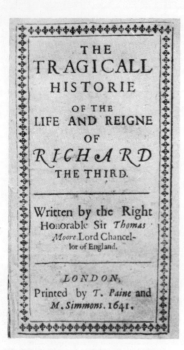

A title page to Sir Thomas More's 'Richard III'. What seems unusual about this page?

John Green with a letter to Sir Robert Brackenbury, Constable of the Tower of London, ordering him to put the boys to death. Sir Robert refused . . . but the King was told by his page that Sir James Tyrrel would do the deed. Now Sir James had watched with envy as others rose above him in the King's favour and . . . agreed to do the deed. He was then sent to Brackenbury with a letter to say that he should be given all the keys of the Tower for one night. The two princes were under the care of Will Slater, called 'Black Will' and Miles Forest, and these two with Sir James Tyrrel and his groom, John Dighton, smothered the princes in their beds. Tyrrel then ordered the murderers to bury them at the foot of the stairs, deep in the ground, under a great heap of stones.

Then rode Sir James to King Richard who gave him great thanks, and as some say, made him a knight. But the king ordered a priest to dig up their bodies and bury them in some other place, because they were the king's sons.

When people give evidence, they are expressing their opinion. The authors of these two chronicles differ on several points. Yet both think that Richard III ordered the murder of his royal nephews.

There are, however, several other important clues in this case.

(3) In the winter of 1483 there was a rumour in England that the princes had died a violent death.

(4) In 1674 some men were digging under a staircase in the Tower. They found a wooden cask with two small skeletons in it. Charles II assumed these were the bones of the princes and placed them in a marble urn in Westminster Abbey.

(5) In 1933 a famous surgeon opened the urn, examined the bones, and said they could have been the remains of the princes. The bloodstain on the skull of one could have been caused by suffocation.

(6) In 1955 a group of doctors and dentists examined photographs of the bones. They concluded they were too young to be the princes. The bloodstain was not caused by suffocation.

(7) Other men also had good reason to kill the princes. The Duke of Buckingham was in London in the summer of 1483 and he was plotting to kill Richard III and put Henry Tudor on the throne. The princes were in his way. He could easily spread the rumour about Richard III to blacken his character.

The historian at work

Did Richard III murder the two young princes? Do we have enough evidence to be sure? The historian must first play the detective. Like Detective Chief Superintendent Butler, he must search for clues, for evidence from archaeology or by 'interviewing' those who wrote at the time. Then he must make up his mind; he must be the prosecuting counsel at the trial or, perhaps, the counsel for the defence. Would you prosecute or defend King Richard?

The making of Christian Europe

The barbarian invasions

The story of Hengist

Imagine a bright spring day by the sea. The sky is clear, the air is fresh and warm, after the long grey cold of winter. The earth is coming back to life. Birds are singing. Green buds appear on the trees.

Look out to sea. A small wooden ship with fourteen banks of oars and one mast is approaching. Before the sail stands a huge figure of a man, Hengist. His bushy beard pushes out from under an iron helmet; his huge chest is covered by chain mail. In his right hand he carries a great sword. Against his leg a round wooden shield rests, at the ready.

As the ship is beached on the shingle, Hengist is the first to leap out, crashing all his weight on the stones. His followers, similarly dressed and armed, quickly follow, their eyes fixed on the land.

This was perhaps how Hengist arrived in England. No one knows for certain that he really existed, but there is a legend that he landed in Kent in AD 449. He may have been invited by a Celtic king called Vortigern, who certainly invited some warriors from Germany to help his own small army. Was Hengist their leader? This is what the *Anglo-Saxon Chronicle* has to say:

They came in three ships to a place called Ebbsfleet (in Kent). King Vortigern gave them lands in the south east on the condition that they fought against the Picts and had many victories over them. They sent news back to Germany to tell their tribes that the land was green and rich, and that the Celts were weak. Soon more came. The Jutes came to Kent, the Old Saxons to the southern part of England and the Angles to the Midlands and Northumbria.

The Picts and Scots were the tribes who lived in what is now Scotland and Ireland. They were defeated by the tribes from Germany. But then these tribes turned on the Celts. The Celtic kings found

A Saxon ship crashes in towards the shore

they were unable to control the armies which they themselves had invited to England and a hundred years later a monk called Gildas described the results:

Every town is battered. Every inhabitant is slaughtered. Priests are put to the sword, towns are put to the flames … some flee to the hills, only to be captured and slain.

In the *Anglo-Saxon Chronicle* again:

In 456, Hengist, the King of Kent, fought against the Celts at Crayford, and there slew four companies. The Celts forsook Kent and fled in great terror.

The Anglo-Saxon Chronicle

Does the *Anglo-Saxon Chronicle* tell us what really happened? It is the earliest account, written in English, which we have of Anglo-Saxon England. The following facts help us to decide whether we can believe what it tells us.

(a) The *Chronicle* was written by several different monks in different monasteries over a very long period of time.

(b) Most of it was written about three hundred years after the events described took place.

(c) It contains almost no detailed information; for example it does not tell us what sort of person Hengist was, or what he looked like.

(d) Other evidence tells the same general story as the *Chronicle*. Blackened pottery found in the ground shows that many houses and other buildings were burnt down in England at this time.

The invaders

The Roman Empire lasted for hundreds of years. As the map overleaf shows, it covered nearly all of Europe as well as much of North Africa and the Near East. A magnificent network of roads, a large army and

A Saxon warrior

The Roman road at Blackstone Edge, as it is today

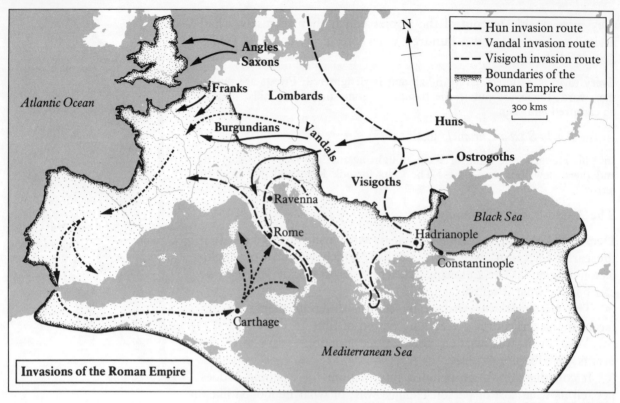

Invasions of the Roman Empire

Map legend:
- Hun invasion route
- Vandal invasion route
- Visigoth invasion route
- Boundaries of the Roman Empire

300 kms

Labels: N, Angles, Saxons, Franks, Lombards, Atlantic Ocean, Burgundians, Vandals, Huns, Ostrogoths, Visigoths, Ravenna, Rome, Hadrianople, Constantinople, Black Sea, Carthage, Mediterranean Sea

A Roman legionary

strong government made this possible. Yet in the fifth and sixth centuries AD the western part of the empire broke up and a number of smaller kingdoms took its place. Only in the eastern Mediterranean did Roman law and customs survive, around the capital city of Constantinople.

From AD 370 onwards a number of tribes, such as the Visigoths and the Huns, moved westwards from central Asia, threatening the Empire. Many of the Roman troops were unused to campaigning and had grown soft, living in garrison towns. In addition, they were heavily outnumbered and often poorly led. Thus they were unable to defeat the invaders.

Throughout their history the Romans had been used to fighting tribes outside their territory. At times they had suffered serious defeats but always they had been victorious in the end. This time they failed and Rome itself was captured and looted several times – first in AD 410. The strongest tribes were the Huns who, under their leader Attila, reached Gaul in 451. The Roman general Aetius was able to defeat them but, as the map shows, his success was purely temporary.

The last Roman soldiers left Britain early in the fifth century AD. The historian Zosimus (writing more than fifty years after the events he is describing) says:

The barbarians across the Rhine attacked everywhere; the peoples of Britain and Gaul decided to revolt from Rome and to obey Roman laws no longer.

The 'barbarians'

These tribes and indeed all foreigners were called 'barbarians' by the Romans. What do we mean by 'barbarian' today? Originally 'barbarian' was a word applied to foreigners because the Romans could not understand what they were saying. (But all the tribes they fought and conquered were described as barbarians and considered as inferior to Roman citizens.) Although generals like Julius Caesar appreciated the fighting skills of the native tribesmen, it was only slowly that non-Italians within the Empire (for example, Spaniards and Gauls) were accepted as full Roman citizens.

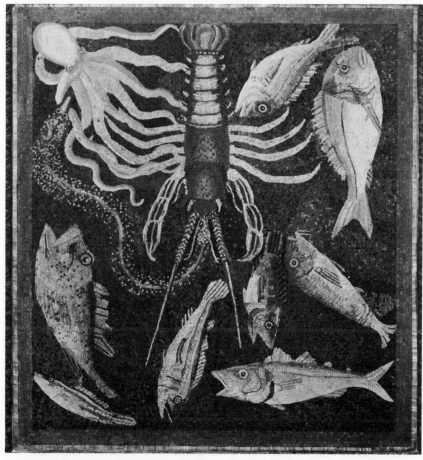

This Roman mosaic was part of a stone floor. It can be seen today in the Victoria and Albert Museum in London.

Not all barbarians were as different from the Romans as the latter liked to make out. When Roman writers described the Huns, for example, they rarely based their comments on first-hand knowledge. Naturally the Huns were very different from the settled, civilised city-dwellers of the Empire. Their raiding caused considerable damage and widespread alarm but the Romans were not always any more restrained when dealing with their opponents. The barbarian tribes were also often as different from one another as from the Romans.

What does the following extract from a Roman writer tell you about his attitude towards the Huns? Find two phrases which it is difficult to believe are true:

They are a very savage people; they all have compact, strong limbs and thick necks, and are so monstrously ugly that one might think them two-legged beasts. . . . They are so hardy that they have no need of fire or savoury food, but eat the roots of wild plants and the half-raw flesh of any wild animal. . . . They are never protected by any buildings, for not even a hut thatched with reed can be found among them. . . . They dress in linen cloth or in skins of fieldmice sewn together; they cover their heads with round caps and protect their hairy legs with goatskins.

The early Saxon kings in England

The Angles, Saxons and Jutes all came to England. At first they formed settlements along the rivers of southern and eastern England (for example Wallingford and Oxford on the Thames). We can tell where these settlements were from the names the Saxons used for villages which still exist today: names ending in *-ing*, *-ton*, *-ford* and *-ham*. Followed by their families, more warriors came over in their long boats. They needed land and took it by force from the Celts.

By around 600, the Angles, Saxons and Jutes had conquered nearly all of present-day England and set up a number of small kingdoms. Eventually three of these kingdoms – Northumbria, Mercia and Wessex – became supreme over the others. The first important overlords or 'bretwaldas' of all Britain were Edwin, Oswald and Oswy, the three great kings of Northumbria between 617 and 657. Then the bretwaldaship passed to the Mercian kings, Ethelbald and Offa who reigned between 731 and 796.

Edwin of Northumbria

The two most famous bretwaldas were Edwin of Northumbria and Offa of Mercia. Edwin won his kingdom in 617 by defeating his brother-in-law, a proud and fierce man called Ethelfrith. He then conquered all the princes of England, except for the powerful king of Kent, whose daughter he married. In addition he accepted a Christian monk called Paulinus into his realm and was himself baptised a Christian. He was only defeated in 633 when a number of princes joined together and killed him in battle. Even so, his kingdom continued under his successors, as you can read in chapter 2.

Offa of Mercia

Offa's first important act was to mint a new type of coin called a penny. It was a large coin with enough space on it for Offa's portrait and the title 'King of Britain'. Offa, in fact, defeated all the British kings south of the Humber, although he never interfered in the affairs of Northumbria, as his daughter was married to Ethelred, its king. He also built the famous Offa's dyke from the estuary of the River Dee to that of the

King Offa of Mercia, from a drawing in a medieval manuscript. What impression of Offa is the artist trying to give?

Severn, to keep the Welsh out of Mercia. Offa issued a great code of laws for his people which King Alfred later used. Such was Offa's fame that after his death he was called the 'King and glory of Britain'.

Offa's Penny

Anglo-Saxon learning

The kingdoms of the Anglo-Saxons produced a number of learned men at a time when there was little learning and education in Europe. There is a story about the Northumbrian poet, Caedmon. He was a simple peasant who, as a young man, attended a celebration in the hall of his village lord. The harp was passed from man to man and each took his turn to sing a song or say a poem. Caedmon could never think of any songs so, as his turn got nearer, he slipped out of the hall and went to a nearby barn where he fell asleep in the hay.

He dreamed that he saw a man who asked him to sing a song about God and the creation of the world. Caedmon had never thought of poems about religious subjects before but he found that he knew the Bible stories so well that poems came easily to him. When he awoke he could remember his poems and later he wrote many others. Anglo-Saxon poetry, in fact, became famous, and it was probably in Mercia at the time of Offa the Great that the epic poem about the legendary warrior Beowulf was written.

The Tassilo Chalice AD 777. This silver-plated cup was carved for Duke Tassilo of Austria by a Saxon metalworker from England.

> That serpent, coiled evilly,
> could no longer guard the gold-hoard,
> but blades of iron, beaten and tempered
> by smiths, notched in battle, had taken him off;
> his wings were clipped now, he lay
> mortally wounded, motionless on the earth
> at the mound's entrance. No more did he fly
> through the night sky, or spread his wings,
> proud of his possessions; but he lay prostrate
> because of the power of Beowulf, their leader.
> *(translation by Kevin Crossley Holland)*

In addition Anglo-Saxon monks wrote chronicles and histories. The greatest of these was written by Bede. Many of the manuscripts were beautifully decorated by the monks. The finds at Sutton Hoo, shown in the Using the evidence section, also illustrate the delicate work with gold, silver and jewellery done at this period.

How do we know?

This book introduces different kinds of evidence. There is less evidence for many of the events described in this chapter than for the later Middle Ages. We also need to look at it more carefully. How do we know what actually happened?

The spoken and written word

Memories of people living at the time are handed down by word of mouth.

Stories grow in the telling – details are forgotten and exaggerations creep in.

Stories are written down, but for a purpose:

perhaps *to entertain*; what actually happened is less important than an exciting story;

perhaps *to instruct*; events and stories are used to support an argument. (Monks, such as Nennius, liked to show that the anger of God fell on evil men, especially those who plundered monasteries.);

perhaps *as history* trying to discover what actually happened, although this is difficult. This often meant recording what seemed to have happened or might have happened.

Archaeological and written evidence are both very valuable. But they tell us different things about the past.

Now look at the legend of King Arthur and the discoveries at Sutton Hoo.

The legend of King Arthur

In the fifth and sixth centuries, it took the Angles, Saxons and Jutes about one hundred and fifty years to conquer Britain. Why did it take so long? Throughout the Middle Ages only one answer was given. Sitting round their fires, men told their children the story of King Arthur. According to legend, Arthur was the son of a Celtic prince. He successfully rallied the Celts against the invaders and won many victories over the Saxons. With his famous sword, Excalibur, he was supposed to have killed many of the enemy him-

Physical remains

Towns, roads, forts, houses, and fields; weapons, tools, jewellery; household utensils, coins.

Damaged, destroyed, buried or overgrown during the centuries. Rediscovered in modern times by archaeologists.

Archaeologists dig and study what they find.
They are able:
  to reconstruct sites, plans of buildings and the activities carried on there – houses, storage buildings, religious buildings;
  to date the buildings and objects they find;
  to build up a picture of the lifestyle, possessions and surroundings of a people or community at a particular time.

Archaeologists at work at Sutton Hoo

self. At Camelot he held a magnificent court and organised tournaments for his knights.

The Arthur legends in the form in which we can read them today date from the Middle Ages. Geoffrey of Monmouth gave a detailed account of King Arthur's reign in his *History of the Kings of Britain*, written in the twelfth century. He based his story on legends and folk-tales from Ireland, Wales, France and other places. When he could find no suitable source to use, Geoffrey used his own imagination freely.

In the fifteenth century Sir Thomas Malory wrote his *Morte d'Arthur*. He invented many of the most famous stories about the wizard, Merlin, and about the knights of the Round Table.

Look at the clues below and decide for yourself how much of the King Arthur legend is true.

(1) In the ninth century a monk called Nennius wrote the following account of a victory over the Saxons. He described the battle as taking place in AD 518; that is, four hundred years earlier.

Arthur's twelfth battle was on Mount Badon. He slew 940 men with his own sword. And in all his battles he was victor. But more Saxons came from Germany to continue the war.

Which sentence of Nennius' is least likely to be true? Which sentence is most likely to be true?

Badbury Rings

(2) Many attempts have been made to find the site of Mount Badon. Badbury Rings in Dorset is one possibility. Archaeologists have found human skeletons and weapons suggesting that there was a battle here at this time.

Does this prove that King Arthur fought in the battle? If not, what further evidence might prove this? Are we likely ever to find this kind of evidence?

(3) Archaeologists have also searched for the site of Camelot. A number of places are linked with King Arthur (for example, Tintagel and Glastonbury in south-west England). However, there is an Arthur's Stone in Glamorgan and also an Arthur's Seat at Edinburgh. Holy relics and the tombs of famous people were the medieval equivalent of the modern tourist attractions. Many poorer as well as wealthy people went on pilgrimages to places like Glastonbury Abbey.

Many objects are also linked with Arthur. But King Arthur's Table, a large round table hanging on a wall in the castle at Winchester, has recently been examined carefully. Analysis of the wood itself and the way in which the table was made indicate that it is no older than the twelfth century.

Why might people of a particular place wish to associate the name of Arthur with their region? Would they have been worried whether their claims were true?

(4) In the mid-sixth century a monk called Gildas wrote an account of *The Destruction and Invasion of Britain*. He clearly indicates a victory over the Saxons in about AD 500. Without such a victory the Saxons would have conquered England more rapidly. The Celts must have had a leader and perhaps his name was Arthur. (Arthur was a Celtic name and Artorius a common Roman one.)

The *Anglo-Saxon Chronicle* though says nothing about King Arthur.

Does the 'Anglo-Saxon Chronicle' give a complete and accurate account of the events of this period (see page 15)?

Using the evidence: the Sutton Hoo ship burial

On the eastern coast of Suffolk, about ten kilometres from the sea and overlooking the estuary of the River Deben stand about fifteen old Anglo-Saxon burial mounds. In 1938 Mrs Edith May Pretty, who owned the land, invited some archaeologists to open up the mounds to see what was inside. They opened three mounds and, in one, found the fragments of a burial boat, an ornamental sword and shield and other possessions. Clearly these were the graves of important men.

Inside the largest mound at Sutton Hoo. What methods have these archaeologists used to avoid damaging their finds?

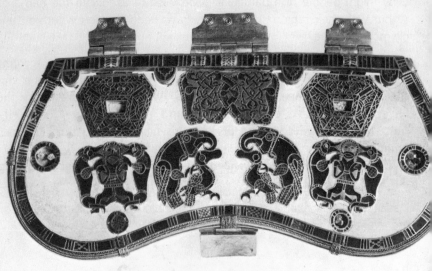

Left The buckle, purse and some coins as they were found by archaeologists in the ground

Right The purse and buckle after they had been cleaned

In the following year Mrs Pretty arranged for the largest of the burial mounds to be opened and the British Museum was called in. The team was led by Mr C. W. Philips, an archaeologist from Cambridge University, and when the digging was completed, the mound was found to contain the outline of a large burial ship and vast wealth in gold, jewels and ornaments. In August 1939 an inquest decided that the finds belonged to Mrs Pretty, but she presented them to the nation and they can now be seen in the British Museum.

The ship and its contents were clearly used in a funeral. The ship was hauled about one hundred metres up from the river and placed in the trench which had been dug for it. The jewels, weapons and other objects placed in the grave were intended to help the dead person in the next world, and the greater the importance of the person the more goods he required. This particular ship contained a great many objects: a sceptre, a small six-stringed lyre, a helmet, and a

This helmet was carefully pieced together from many fragments found in the mound

sword, as well as drinking dishes, spoons, ornamental bowls, a bronze cauldron, a large hoard of coins from all over Europe, and some fine silver and jewelled ornaments which probably included an ivory chess set.

Who was the warrior king buried at Sutton Hoo? Archaeologists can tell from the dates of the coins which were found in the purse that the grave was probably made in 625 and this is also the year when Redwald, the king of East Anglia, died. He was a powerful warrior who was also the bretwalda overlord of the other kingdoms of England. The amazing thing is that his grave and its rich contents lay under the ground undisturbed for over 1300 years!

Questions and further work

1 Read the extract from *Beowulf* on page 19 and the following quotation:
  'Then came the time when Scyld had to go as a warrior into the land of the dead'.
  How does this written evidence help the archaeologist to understand what he found at Sutton Hoo?
2 Which of the findings do you think was the most helpful to date the Sutton Hoo burial?
3 Make a list of the things that the archaeologists found at Sutton Hoo. Why did they have to be careful when uncovering their find?
4 What can we learn about the man who was buried in the ship? Which finds especially help you to decide about him?
5 The Huns, according to the writer on page 18, were a 'very savage people'. List all the main points from his description. Then reread the evidence about the Anglo-Saxons in the Sutton Hoo evidence section. Were all barbarians as savage as the Roman writer would lead us to believe?
6 Imagine you were a mourner at the burial of King Redwald in 625. Describe the preparations for the funeral as you saw them. Why would various things like the objects found in the Sutton Hoo mound be placed in his mound?

The sceptre

2 Europe becomes Christian

The story of Saint Alban

In the Roman town of Verulamium, thirty-two kilometres north of London, there lived a handsome and wealthy young nobleman called Alban. One day, after he had been out visiting some friends, Alban returned to his house to find a feeble and weary old man, hiding by the door. The old man said he was Amphibalus, a Christian priest, and that he was being pursued by Roman soldiers. Alban took pity on him. He gave Amphibalus food and sheltered him for several days. Often he stopped to listen to the priest's stories about Jesus.

During one of their meetings they were interrupted by the noise of soldiers. Quickly Alban gave the old man money and showed him a secret way out. Alban himself then dressed in the priest's clothes. When the soldiers entered the house, they arrested him and took him before the governor.

The governor still recognised Alban and offered to pardon him if he would offer a sacrifice to the Roman gods. Alban, however, refused, saying that there was only one God, the God of the Christians. The governor then ordered Alban to be executed.

At Alban's execution a remarkable thing is said to have happened.

St Alban being led to his execution

Before the sword came down, Alban asked for a drink of water and suddenly a 'spring of fair-flowing water' emerged from the ground. On seeing this the executioner threw down his sword, saying, 'I cannot do it, for here is a holy man.' The Roman governor then ordered Alban and his executioner to be killed together. Many men who heard the tale marvelled at Alban's bravery and became Christian themselves.

Fact or fiction?

After the death of Jesus Christ, Christian teaching slowly spread throughout the Roman Empire. In 303 the Emperor Diocletian 'commanded that all Christians should be tortured and killed, and that their churches should be burned and destroyed'. In parts of the Empire individual Christians showed great courage in facing the emperor's soldiers and officials. The Roman army in Britain had orders to hunt down Christians. Sometimes they showed little mercy.

The story of St Alban comes largely from the *Ecclesiastical History* written by the monk Bede. But if we compare it with the stories written by other monks at the time, we can see that Bede made many errors:

(a) Bede tells of a miracle: water gushes from the ground. But this story was a very common one at this time. It is fiction.

(b) The name Amphibalus is not given in other accounts. How did Bede know it?

(c) Bede says the events took place a century later than they did.

Religious beliefs

During the next two hundred years, the numbers of Christians in Europe as a whole did not increase very much. Most men believed there were many gods, rather than just one. The Romans worshipped their gods in huge and splendid temples: gods like Mars, who gave them victory in war, and Venus, the goddess who made their crops grow. The Angles and Saxons had similar gods of their own: Woden, the chief of all gods; Thunor, the god of thunder, and Frig, who, like Venus, brought a good harvest. Saxon kings placed images of the gods they worshipped on the altars of their temples. Before a battle they would go into the temple to pray to Woden for victory. Like many other peoples, the Saxons also believed in magic, giants and monsters. But they also believed that when a man died, he went on a long journey to another world beyond the grave. This description of a funeral comes from the story of the great warrior Beowulf:

Then the people constructed a splendid pyre on the ground, hung with helmets and war-shields, and in the middle the lamenting warriors laid the body of their prince. Then the warriors began to light the wood and the smoke rose high, black above the pyre. The roaring flame mingled with the weeping until it had burned the wood and the body. Then the people built a high barrow or mound on the cliff so that it could be seen afar by seafarers . . . and they laid jewels and rings on the barrow.

Although most men in northern Europe still believed in the old gods,

Iona Abbey today. In the background is the island of Mull.

many in the south were being influenced by the teachings of Jesus Christ. After Jesus had been crucified in Jerusalem, many of his followers sailed overseas to preach. St Paul went on many journeys throughout the Mediterranean. St Peter is said to have gone to Rome where he converted many people and became the city's first bishop. Soon after, the bishop of Rome became known as the Pope or Father, and became the leader of the Christian Church. Missionaries travelled from Rome across the Alps to the north and west. Two important centres of Christianity developed – one among the Franks of Gaul, the other among the Celts (living in western Britain and Ireland). In time, though, the whole of Europe became influenced by Christianity. For much of the Middle Ages, therefore, men described Europe itself as 'Christendom'.

Clovis and the Franks

In 496 Clovis, king of the Franks, was baptised as a Christian. He had married Clotilda, the Christian daughter of the king of Burgundy. She urged Clovis to recognise the true God and cease worshipping idols. However, it was said that he was only really persuaded during a battle against a rival tribe called the Alemanni. The Franks appeared to be losing. Clovis was afraid. He prayed to his gods, but still his men were being killed. In desperation, he then cried to Jesus Christ: 'I promise that if you will grant me victory over these enemies . . . I will believe in you and be baptised in your name.' Suddenly, according to the legend, the Alemanni turned and fled. Clovis and his people became Christians.

As a result the Franks became the protectors of the Christian faith and, for the next four hundred years, the friends and allies of the pope. It was a Frank, Charles Martel (Charles the Hammer), who defended Christendom by defeating the Moslems at Poitiers in 732.

Missionaries and saints

St Ninian and St Patrick

The second group of Christians in northern Europe at this time were the Celts of Britain, the tribes who were defeated by the Anglo-Saxons and driven into Wales, Cumberland and Ireland. About the year 400, St Ninian became the first Christian bishop in England, with his church at Whithorn in Cumberland. According to tradition St Patrick may have lived near there as a child. He was captured by raiders and taken as a slave to Ireland. Later he escaped, went to Rome and became a bishop. On his return to Ireland in 432 he converted the people to Christianity.

Patrick and his fellow Christians founded many monasteries in Cornwall, South Wales and Ireland. In 563 the great monastery at Iona, off the Scottish coast, was established by St Columba.

Pope Gregory the Great

Gregory, the son of a rich nobleman, was born about 540, at a time when Italy was being raided by several different barbarian tribes. 'Rome is deserted and in flames and her buildings are all in ruins,' he wrote. First the Goths invaded, then the fierce and warlike Lombards. The Roman people were torn by plague, poverty and war. When Gregory's father died, Gregory became wealthy, but he decided to sell all his land and use the money to build six monasteries where people could seek refuge from war. Even his own house in Rome became a monastery and the monks lived according to the rules of St Benedict (see chapter 14).

In 590 Gregory became pope. In the next fourteen years he tried to make the Roman Church important to all men in Europe. He kept in close touch with archbishops and bishops and sent them many letters. He even wrote a book called *The Shepherd's Care* to instruct them.

Gregory was also a saintly and kindly pope. He gave most of his money to the poor beggars of Rome and helped to nurse people who were sick with the plague. He even organised soldiers to defend the city against invaders. Through his efforts, the Christian church became accepted throughout Europe. One of his most successful ventures was to send monks under Augustine to England to convert the Saxons.

St Augustine and the Saxons

In 597 St Augustine and his followers landed on the Isle of Thanet off the coast of Kent. Ethelbert, the king of Kent, had a Christian wife, so he knew about Christianity before the monks came. At first, however, he was suspicious of them. He received them in the open air 'so that they should not practise any magical art in any house and so get the better of him'. Yet he gave them a house in Canterbury and allowed them to preach to the people. In time Ethelbert was baptised and his kingdom became Christian. Augustine was made the first archbishop of Canterbury in 601. He was given power by Pope Gregory to appoint a further twelve English bishops.

St Paulinus, depicted on a stained glass window at York Minster

Christianity gradually spread northwards and in 625 a monk named Paulinus was encouraged to convert the people of Northumbria. Two years later he met King Edwin of Northumbria and his nobles. The king asked his counsellors for their views and was persuaded to become a Christian by this wise speech:

Sire, when we think of this present life of ours, and then compare it with the great stretch of time that comes before and after, about which we know nothing, it brings a picture to my mind. I see a sparrow flying swiftly through the king's hall on a winter's day. Inside there is a warm comforting fire, but outside the snow and hail are raging. The sparrow flies quickly in at one door, through the hall and out of the other door. While he is inside, he is safe, warm and comforted – but only for a brief moment. Then he is gone again, out of our sight into the darkness.

It is just the same for us. We are on Earth for a very short time. We know nothing of what happened before or what will happen after. And so if there is anything we can learn from this new teaching, then we should follow it.

Paulinus was then made the first bishop of York. But when Edwin was killed in battle in 633, Northumbria again lapsed into the old heathen ways.

St Columba's missionaries

It was at this point that the Celtic missionaries arrived from Iona. Columba had had the courage to sail across the Irish Sea in an open boat to preach to Buda, king of the Picts (the tribe who lived in what is now Scotland). Then Columba's follower, Aidan, was sent south in 635 to restore Northumbria to Christianity.

Aidan was a gentle, humble man. He tried to talk simply to the ordinary people 'just as children are fed on milk before they can eat meat. Then they are taught the more difficult parts of Christ's faith when they are able to understand it.' Aidan became a friend and adviser of King Oswald and founded the great monastery on Lindisfarne or Holy Island. He helped Oswald and his successor, Oswy, to build other monasteries and defeat the heathen Mercians in battle.

St Cuthbert. Whose head is he carrying?

After his death in 651 Aidan was followed by St Cuthbert, a tall strong shepherd lad who had become a monk at Melrose. He wandered through Northumbria preaching and teaching the people in a simple way. Once, on a cold winter's night, he and a young friend could find no shelter or food. The boy was extremely hungry but Cuthbert was sure that God would provide something to eat. Suddenly an eagle came swooping down and dropped a large fish nearby. Cuthbert cut the fish in half, threw half to the eagle, and gave the other half to his companion. Stories of such miracles helped many to believe that men like Cuthbert and Aidan were saints.

The Whitby meeting

The Roman and Celtic monks converted many people in England to Christianity. However, for over two hundred years, Celtic monks had been separated from the rest of the church. As a result they had developed their own customs. They had a different date for Easter, a different service for baptism and their monks even had a different tonsure (haircut). Most important of all, Celtic monks did not accept that the pope at Rome should be the leader of the Church. In King Oswy's own household there were differences. (He was a Celtic Christian and his wife was a Roman Christian from Kent.)

In 664, Oswy held a meeting of churchmen at Whitby Abbey to decide whether to accept Roman practices or keep to the Celtic ones. After much discussion, the meeting agreed with Oswy to follow Roman practices. The whole of England thus became part of the Catholic (which means *universal*) Church.

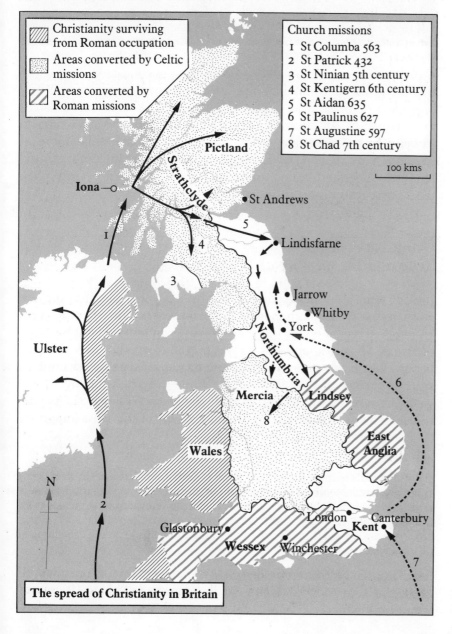

Christianity surviving from Roman occupation

Areas converted by Celtic missions

Areas converted by Roman missions

Church missions

1 St Columba 563
2 St Patrick 432
3 St Ninian 5th century
4 St Kentigern 6th century
5 St Aidan 635
6 St Paulinus 627
7 St Augustine 597
8 St Chad 7th century

100 kms

Pictland

Strathclyde

Iona

St Andrews

Lindisfarne

Jarrow

Whitby

York

Ulster

Northumbria

Mercia

Lindsey

East Anglia

Wales

N

London

Canterbury

Kent

Glastonbury

Wessex

Winchester

The spread of Christianity in Britain

*The Saxon church at Escomb,
County Durham*

The Ruthwell Cross

Bishoprics were set up and schools helped to educate young men to become priests and missionaries. Two such missionaries were Willibrord and Boniface, who helped to convert the Germans and Frisians to Christianity. In addition, although many people were forced to worship in the open air, some churches were built like those at Escomb, York, Ripon and Hexham. This Christian learning, centred in Northumberland, lasted for nearly two hundred years. Only when the Vikings came, was it destroyed.

Using the evidence:
Bede and the meeting at Whitby (664)

Just ten years after the meeting at Whitby, a boy was born near the new monastery at Wearmouth (now in Tyne and Wear). When he was seven, his father, a tenant on the monastery lands, sent him to the abbot to be educated. Shortly afterwards he was moved to another new abbey at Jarrow. The boy's name was Bede and he remained at Jarrow until his death at the age of sixty-two in 735. While there he wrote over forty books, the greatest of which was his *Ecclesiastical History of the English People*. This was finished in 731 and was one of the most important books written in the Middle Ages.

In his preface to the book, Bede wrote:

(1) With God's help, I, Bede, the servant of Christ and priest of the monastery at Jarrow, have assembled these facts about the history of the Christian Church in Britain, as I have been able to learn them from ancient documents, from listening to old men talk, and from my own personal knowledge. . . . For if history records good things of good men, the thoughtful reader is encouraged to copy what is good.

As he lived in Northumbria Bede had difficulty in finding out about St Augustine's mission to Kent, so he contacted Abbot Albinus of Canterbury who:

The Monk Bede in his scriptorium. Notice his pen.

(2) Carefully learned from written records or from old traditions all that the monks had done in the kingdom of Kent or in the neighbouring kingdoms. Whatever seemed worth remembering he passed on to me through Nothelm, a godly priest, either in writing or by word of mouth.

The following accounts are typical of Bede's writing. The first described the victory of Oswald, the Christian king of Northumbria, over the heathen king Cadwallon, at the battle of Heavenfield in 633. Oswald was heavily outnumbered but on the eve of the battle:

(3) he prayed to the Lord on bended knees that he should help his worshippers in the fight. It is said that a wooden cross was then quickly made and a hole prepared in the ground. The king himself, fervent in his belief, took the cross in his own hands and placed it in the ground, while the soldiers heaped dirt upon it. And when this was done he cried out aloud to the whole army, 'Let us all pray to Almighty God to defend us from this cruel enemy.' All did as he commanded and in the dawning of the day they marched forward against the enemy, and, because they had faith in God, they achieved the victory. And in the place where they prayed, many works of healing are known to have been performed.

Bede's *History* also described the meeting of churchmen at Whitby in 664 to decide whether the Celts should follow the Roman church. (Remember that Bede was born only ten years after this event.)

(4) There were present at the meeting the king Oswy; on the Celtic side, Colman, the bishop with his clergy; and on the Roman side, Agilbert, the bishop, with Wilfrid and other priests. . . .

King Oswy first made an opening speech in which he said that, since they all

The abbey church at Whitby

worshipped the same Christian God, so they all ought to practise the same customs and ceremony in their churches. He then commanded bishop Colman to declare what customs the Celtic Church followed.

Colman said: 'The date of Easter which I keep I received from my elders and they were all men beloved of God. It is the same date which John the Evangelist, the disciple specially loved by Christ, celebrated.'

Then the king ordered Wilfrid to speak and he said: 'The Easter date which we keep is the one celebrated by all at Rome, where the blessed Apostles Peter and Paul lived, taught, suffered and were buried. The same is kept in Italy, Gaul, Africa, Egypt and Greece and all the world, except only for these Picts and Northumbrians.

'But these Celts certainly sin if they fail to follow the decrees of the Bishop of Rome. . . . And if that Columba of yours was a holy man who performed powerful miracles, could he be more important than St Peter, to whom Jesus Christ said, "Thou art Peter and upon thee will I build my Church."?'

When Wilfrid had ended his speech, King Oswy asked, 'Is it true, Colman, that Jesus said these words to St Peter?' and Colman replied that it was true. Then Oswy said, 'Can you show me that anything like that was ever said to Columba?' And Colman replied that he could not. The king therefore decided that St Peter's Church was the true Church and all who were seated there or standing by gave their agreement and Roman customs were accepted all over the land.

Questions and further work

1 Look again at the list on pages 20 and 21. List these things in the order of importance that they had for Bede.
2 From what sources did Bede obtain his information? Which of these do you think was the most reliable, and why?
3 Why might information passed on by Abbot Albinus have been inaccurate or misleading?
4 Now that you have considered why Bede wrote his book and how he got his information, say which of these statements are probably correct, and which are probably incorrect.
(a) The site of the Battle of Heavenfield became a place where people went to be healed.
(b) Oswald's army won the battle because they believed in God.
(c) King Oswald erected a cross on the battlefield.
(d) Before 664 all countries in the known world, except Northumbria, celebrated Easter on the same date as Rome.
(e) After the meeting at Whitby, King Oswy believed that St Peter was more important than St Columba.
5 Imagine you were a Celtic monk supporting Colman at Whitby. Describe the meeting as you saw it and your own feelings about what happened.
6 What did the monks do once they had decided at Whitby which church practices to follow? Can you suggest a reason why the north of England became their centre, rather than the south, which is nearer to Rome?

3 The Mediterranean world

The Roman Empire of Justinian (527–65)

By the sixth century the vast empire of Ancient Rome had been torn apart. In the west, invading tribes had built up kingdoms: the Vandals in North Africa, the Goths in Spain and Italy and the Franks to the north of the Alps.

In the east, however, the Roman Empire still survived. Its capital was the huge, rich city of Constantinople. In AD 518 the commander of the palace guard, a former peasant called Justin, made himself emperor. After nine years he died and was followed by his nephew Justinian. With his wife, Theodora, Justinian tried to restore the great empire of old.

The first step was to reconquer the old Empire in Italy and the west. In 533 their general Belisarius defeated the Vandals and conquered North Africa. He then sailed over to Italy and captured both Rome and Ravenna. But the Empire was harder to hold than it was to conquer. The long sea voyage between Constantinople and Rome made it difficult to keep troops and supplies in Italy; Justinian also never really trusted Belisarius and refused to give him wholehearted support. Soon most of Italy had been reconquered by the invading Lombards.

It was in the east that Justinian's influence was really felt. He and his advisers completely reorganised the whole of Roman law so that any quarrel could be quickly decided. The *Corpus Juris Civilis* or 'Body of Civil Law' which he published formed a basis for laws which still exist in many parts of the world today. His other great achievement was in the buildings of Constantinople. The magnificent Church of Sancta Sophia (Holy Wisdom) with its marble and mosaics in beautiful colours, well-lit by the bright sunlight, is a tribute to this great emperor.

The Emperor Justinian

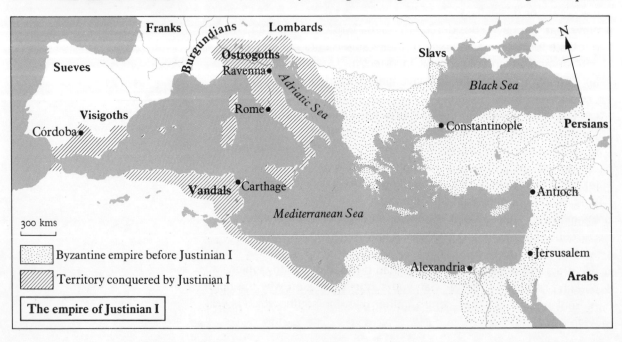

Franks · Burgundians · Lombards · Sueves · Ostrogoths · Ravenna · Slavs · Black Sea · Visigoths · Córdoba · Rome · Adriatic Sea · Constantinople · Persians · Vandals · Carthage · Mediterranean Sea · Antioch · Jerusalem · Alexandria · Arabs

300 kms

Byzantine empire before Justinian I

Territory conquered by Justinian I

The empire of Justinian I

The great cathedral church of Sancta Sophia. It is now a Moslem mosque.

Yet Justinian's empire was never easy to hold. There was always the threat of murder or assassination, and the mob of Constantinople was a particular problem. At the Hippodrome, there were regular chariot races and other sporting occasions. Many spectators attended, and there were two chariot teams belonging to the main political parties, the Blues and the Greens. In Constantinople at that time you supported either one or the other. Supporters of the Blues had short beards and partially-shaved heads. They wore wide sleeved tunics and close-fitting stockings and shoes but the Greens, by contrast, were not bothered about their appearance. Rivalry between the two teams was so fierce that they even attended different churches.

While Justin was emperor the mob became very unruly. So in 532 Justinian decided to punish them severely. But the rioting only got worse and so he gave orders to make an example of seven men found guilty of murder. Three were sentenced to hang, but two of the ropes were faulty and one Green and one Blue fell to the ground still alive. Some monks rescued them and took them to the safety of a nearby monastery.

The next day there was a large race-meeting at the Hippodrome. As usual Justinian and Theodora attended. The two sides began to chant 'Nika . . . Nika' ('Victory . . . Victory') together. A riot started and Justinian had to flee for safety. The mob broke into prisons, killed guards, set buildings on fire. The cathedral, the senate house and even parts of the royal palace were ablaze. Justinian thought that the only sensible move was to flee. But apparently he changed his mind, because his wife, Theodora, is said to have thrown herself before her husband:

The Empress Theodora

It is impossible for a man, once he has been born, not to die. But for a King it is intolerable to be an exile. May I never see the day when I am not called 'Queen'. If you wish, O Emperor, to save yourself, there is money and there are ships. But . . . I prefer death to safety.

Justinian is said to have gained fresh courage from her words and his general Belisarius finally dispersed the crowds and restored order.

The Persian Wars

After Justinian's death his successors became involved with another large empire in the east, that of the Persians. This stretched from the Mediterranean to India and between 606 and 628 there was a fierce war between its ruler Chosroes II and the Roman (or Byzantine) Emperor Heraclius. The Persians were successful at first. They captured Syria and Egypt, and in 614 massacred over 57 000 Christians at Jerusalem, then carried off the True Cross, on which Christ was said to have been crucified. Heraclius, however, fought back and defeated Chosroes, recovering Egypt and Syria and weakening the Persian Empire. In the process he recaptured the Cross and in turn massacred the Jews of Jerusalem who had helped the Persians in 614. The war, of course, weakened both empires, and although the Byzantines had won, they were hated by their subject peoples, who had to pay heavy taxes to them. There was, therefore, no strong united power to oppose the Arab tribesmen who answered the call of the Prophet Mohammed to a 'Holy War'.

The story of Mohammed (570–632)

Mohammed was born in the desert city of Mecca about the year 570. He never knew his father, who died before he was born, and when he was six his mother also died. Mohammed (the name means 'highly praised') grew up in the humble house of his uncle. He did various odd jobs, looking after sheep and selling goods in the market. Then he became an agent for a wealthy widow called Khadija: she was impressed with his gentle and loyal personality (he was nicknamed 'trustworthy'), and by his burly appearance and intelligence.

When Mohammed was twenty-five, Khadija asked him to marry her. Even though she was fifteen years his senior he accepted. She bore him seven children, and they lived happily until her death. Often Mohammed would go into a cave on nearby Mount Hira to pray, and one day in 610 a strange event took place.

The Angel Gabriel came to him and told him to preach the word of God. When Mohammed replied that he could not do it, the angel took a long piece of cloth and began to choke him with it. This happened three times until Mohammed agreed. . . . 'I awoke from my sleep,' said Mohammed, 'and it was as if a message were written in my heart. I heard the voice of Gabriel again and looked up and saw him in the form of a man on the horizon. He moved neither backward nor forward, yet whichever way I turned I continued to see him on the horizon.'

After his call, Mohammed had a number of other dreams and immediately after each one, he recited God's message to his followers, who wrote down God's word in the Koran, the Moslem holy book.

Mohammed's message soon spread through Mecca and then over a wider area of Arabia. The rulers of Mecca, however, were annoyed by his attack on the gods they believed in and by 622 it was no longer safe for him to stay there. In that year, therefore, he and his followers left Mecca and moved 450 kilometres north-east to Medina, where many men had already been converted by his message. This journey is known as the 'Hegira', the 'beginning of new life', and it marks the start of the Moslem calendar in the same way that the birth of Christ marks the beginning of the Christian one.

Mohammed preaching in Medina,
from a fourteenth-century manuscript

At Medina, Mohammed built up an army of loyal followers and in 628 he marched south, conquered Mecca and made it the centre of the new religion. One of the major religions of the world had been born. In the centuries after his death the Islamic religion was to spread to many different countries, and to be accepted by many millions of people.

Islam

The word 'Islam' means 'submission to the will of God'. Moslem faith has five pillars or central parts: faith, prayer, almsgiving, fasting and pilgrimage. This faith is revealed to man in the Koran. Every Moslem must declare that he believes in the one God, Allah: 'There is no god but Allah, and Mohammed is his prophet' (*La ilaha illa Allah; Mohammed rasul Allah*'). Secondly, all Moslems must pray regularly and usually alone to Allah. They should do this five times each day, reciting their prayers as they kneel facing towards Mecca. Once a week (on Fridays) they should attend public worship in a mosque, where the prayers are led by the *imam* or prayer-leader. Thirdly, they should give alms to the poor, as Chapter 271 of the Koran states:

If you give alms openly it is well. If you hide it and give it to the poor secretly it is even better; for Allah sees all you do.

The Moslem should also fast during daytime for one month of the year, and at least once in his life he should go on a special pilgrimage to Mecca. The Koran also shows Moslems how to behave. They should not eat pork since the pig is considered an unclean animal. They should not give false weight when trading. They should avoid strong drink and gambling, 'for in both there is great sin'.

Finally all Moslems were encouraged to fight a holy war, called a 'Jihad', against unbelievers, in order to convert them to Islam. The first Holy War was that fought by Mohammed against the people of Mecca and before his death the prophet had planned to march north into Syria.

The conquests of Islam

During the years after the prophet's death, the poorly-armed Arab horsemen gradually conquered most of the land from the Mediterranean Sea to India. At first their armies were small. They were poorly armed and disorganised, and had no battle plans. When they attacked Syria, the Emperor Heraclius treated them with contempt. He had just defeated the great Persian Empire and considered these Arab horsemen no real threat, so he left Syria and returned to Constantinople. By 638, however, the Moslems had conquered Syria. By 644 they had overrun Persia and were riding into India. At the same time they were turning their attention westwards, conquering Egypt in 642. With the help of North African Berbers or Moors they captured the old Vandal kingdom and in 711 marched into Spain. In spite of all the odds, their armies had been remarkably successful.

Now, however, two major defeats halted their progress. In 717 after a

Mohammed leads his followers on a 'Jihad'

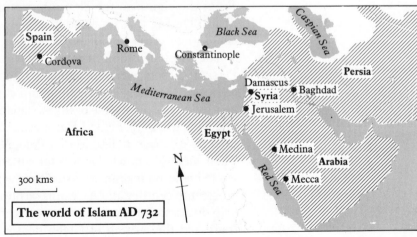

The Kaaba in Mecca. Moslems from all parts of the world visit the Kaaba to pray.

The world of Islam AD 732

bitter battle they were driven back from the walls of Constantinople. In the west, after marching through Spain and across the Pyrenees into France they were defeated in 732 by Charles Martel, King of the Franks, at the Battle of Poitiers.

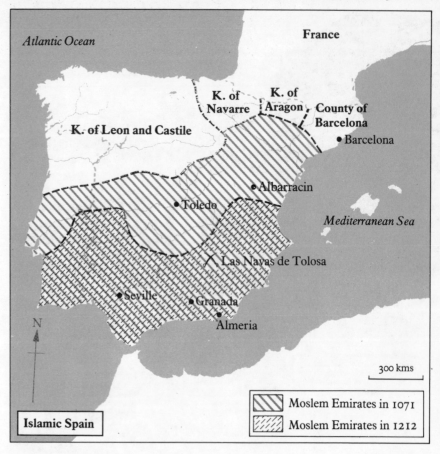

Atlantic Ocean

France

K. of Navarre

K. of Aragon

County of Barcelona

• Barcelona

K. of Leon and Castile

• Albarracin

• Toledo

Mediterranean Sea

Las Navas de Tolosa

• Seville

• Granada

• Almeria

N

300 kms

Islamic Spain

Moslem Emirates in 1071
Moslem Emirates in 1212

Moslem Spain

From the eighth to the eleventh century the Moslems ruled most of Spain. During that time and after they passed on the benefits of their civilisation to the rest of Europe.

The Moslem Empire traded as far east as China and new silks and Persian carpets were introduced into the West. So, too, were the compass, the skills of irrigation and cattle breeding and a number of new foods and plants like oranges, bananas, sugar, and even the English rose. Their travels helped Europeans to make maps which were later used by discoverers like Marco Polo, Vasco da Gama and Columbus. Their medical knowledge was far superior to that of the West: Rhazes wrote books on measles and smallpox which were still being used in the nineteenth century and Avicenna wrote a great medical encyclopedia to help doctors; they had great surgeons and eye-specialists and they also translated the writing of Greek doctors like Galen and Hippocrates. Their mathematical knowledge gave Europe the arabic numbers which we use today, including the important zero. In music too, we owe much to the Arabs; they introduced string instruments like the guitar. Finally, the stories they wrote, such as the two hundred tales of adventure in the *Arabian Nights*, are still read today.

527	Justinian comes to power
565	Death of Justinian
614	Chosroes II seizes Jerusalem
622	Mohammed fled from Mecca to Medina
628	Reconquest of Mecca by Mohammed
628	Heraclius reconquers Jerusalem
717	Moslems defeated at Constantinople
732	Moslems defeated at Poitiers

The door of a mosque at Fez in Morocco

A carved ivory casket from Cordova

Using the evidence: the Battle of Poitiers (732)

Here is one account of the battle written at the time.

(1) Near the River Loire, the two great armies were set out against each other. The Moslems were the first to begin the fight; their horsemen dashed fiercely and frequently against the battalions of the Franks who resisted manfully. Many fell dead on either side until the going down of the sun. Night parted the two armies, but in the grey of early morning, the Moslems returned to battle and their brave horsemen had soon cut their way into the centre of the Christian host.

Then, suddenly, a false cry went around the Moslem knights that some of the enemy were robbing the camp of all the spoil and plunder they had taken so far. Therefore several Moslem squadrons rode back to protect the camp. However, it seemed to the others that they had fled and all the army was troubled. While Abderrahman, the Moslem general, was trying to rally his men, the Franks rode in on him and he was pierced through with many spears and he died. Then all the host fled before the Franks.

Charles Martel enters Paris in triumph after his victory at Poitiers

Here are three summaries of the battle, written by modern historians.

(2) One of the most important leaders was Abdal-Rahman. . . . He gathered an army of 80 000 men and marched into France where he was met by the army of Charles Martel between Tours and Poitiers. An initial and undecisive skirmish took place, lasting almost a week. Abdal-Rahman perished on the battlefield. Facing the serious loss of its leader, the Arab army fled by night. . . .

This rather uneventful confrontation is often considered one of the greatest battles in the world. Muslim historians, usually inclined towards details, hardly mention it. The Arab withdrawal from Tours was not the first of its kind. The Arabs may have learned that intrusion into France was not profitable enough, because of the terrain, climate, distance from supplies, and the unsettled situation in Spain.

A. G. Chejne, Muslim Spain (1974)

(3) New waves of conquest swirled deep into France, as far as Poitiers. Here Charles Martel at last broke the invaders. He preserved Europe from Muslim domination.

E. Hole, Andalus (1958)

(4) The battle has been regarded as one of the decisive contests in history, on the supposition that, had the Moslems won, the whole of Gaul would have been theirs.

J. F. O'Callaghan, Medieval Spain (1975)

Questions and further work

1 How does the author of Document 1 explain the defeat of the Moslems? How does he explain the fact that they turned and ran?
2 What can you tell from Document 1 about its author? Was he a Moslem or a Christian? Give the evidence for your answer.
3 How does the author of Document 2 explain the Moslem defeat and flight? How does it differ from Document 1?
4 Why do the authors of Documents 3 and 4 think the battle was important?
5 What reasons does the author of Document 2 give for suggesting that the battle was not important?
6 In Documents 3 and 4 it is suggested that the Moslems would have conquered all of Gaul had they won the battle of Poitiers. Read Documents 1 and 2 again to see if you can find further evidence to support this view.

Charlemagne

The Great Christian Emperor

One day Charlemagne, the king of the German tribe called the Franks, was visiting a great cathedral when a 'certain wandering monk' came in and found he could not sing the chant with the other monks. The choirmaster threatened to hit him with his baton if he did not sing, so the monk moved his lips but made no noise, hoping to deceive everyone. The other choir monks all roared with laughter. Charlemagne took pity on his confusion, thanked him for his singing, and ordered him to be given a pound of silver to relieve his poverty.

This story was told by a Frankish monk, Notker the Stammerer.

Monks singing in the choir. Describe their dress. Are they enjoying their singing?

The name Charlemagne comes from the Latin words *Carolus Magnus*, 'Charles the Great'. He reigned over the Franks from 768 to 814 and conquered a huge empire. Yet he also began a great revival of education, learning, writing and building in Christian Europe.

Charlemagne's biographer, Einhard, gives us a vivid description of the emperor:

He was strong and well-built. He was tall in stature but not excessively so . . . the top of his head was round and his eyes were piercing and unusually large. He had a fine head of white hair and his expression was gay and good-humoured. As a result, he always appeared masterful and dignified. His neck was short and rather thick and his stomach a trifle too heavy, but the proportions of the rest of his body prevented one from noticing these small blemishes.

His step was firm and he was manly in all his movements. . . . His health was good except that he suffered from frequent attacks of fever during his last four years and towards the end he was lame in one foot. . . . He spent much of his time on horseback and he loved hunting. . . . He was an extremely strong swimmer and in this sport no one could surpass him.

What words tell you that Einhard admired Charlemagne? What faults did Einhard say he had?

How do we know?

Our knowledge comes largely from biographies (life stories) that were written soon after Charlemagne's death. Einhard was a member of the court. Naturally his account of his master's life would be biased in Charlemagne's favour. Other biographers like Notker recorded many of the legends which, though probably untrue, spread around Europe after the emperor's death. To balance these writings we have Charlemagne's own laws or edicts and many letters written by him or about him.

Charlemagne's empire

The Franks

The Franks were one of the barbarian tribes who invaded the weakened Roman Empire in the fifth century and conquered most of northern Gaul. Charlemagne's two predecessors, Charles Martel and his son Pepin the Short, were both powerful rulers. Charles defeated the Moslem invaders at the battle of Poitiers in 732 and added southern Gaul, Aquitaine, to the Frankish kingdom. Pepin continued to defend western Europe against the Moslems and to support the pope. The alliance was confirmed when Pope Stephen visited Pepin and his sons in Gaul. Pepin then defeated Aistulf, the Lombard king of Italy, and gave his lands to the pope. He also drove the Moslems out of France and forced Aquitaine to accept Frankish rule. In 768, on his death, his lands were shared between two brothers, Charlemagne and Carloman, but the latter died in 771, leaving Charlemagne the sole ruler of the Frankish kingdom.

Charlemagne with Pope Leo III and one of his bishops. In what way is this picture like the one of Offa on page 18? Note the very delicate carving.

The conquests of Charlemagne

Charlemagne was eager to add to Pepin's kingdom. By 814 his empire was huge. It ranged from the River Ebro in Spain to the River Elbe in Germany, and from the Atlantic Ocean in the north to Italy in the south. He defeated the Saxons after years of hard fighting and cruelty on both sides. After 782 many Saxons were forced to leave their homes, accept Christian baptism and live among the Franks in Gaul. They became part of the Frankish nation, paying regular taxes, and sometimes fighting in Charlemagne's army.

Charlemagne also attacked the disloyal Duke Tassilo of Bavaria. According to Einhard, Tassilo 'went in person to beg the king's forgiveness and handed over his own son as hostage'. He was forbidden ever to set foot in Bavaria again and the land was thereafter ruled by

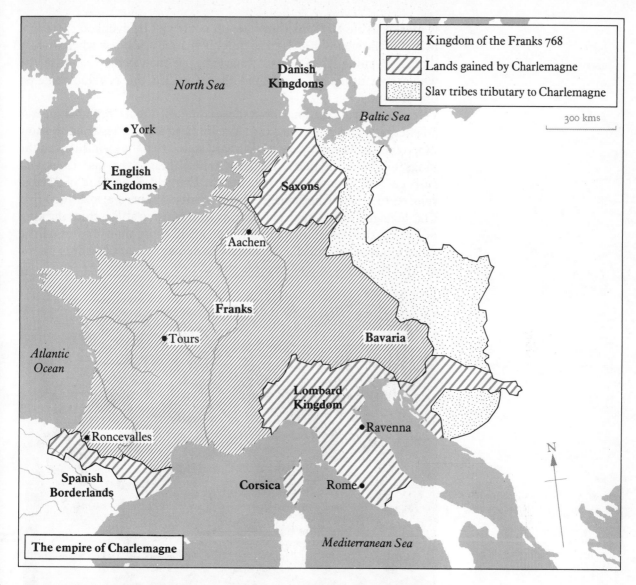

The empire of Charlemagne

Legend:
- Kingdom of the Franks 768
- Lands gained by Charlemagne
- Slav tribes tributary to Charlemagne

300 kms

Charlemagne. The Slavs were also conquered. 'A single campaign, which the king directed himself, sufficed to tame them, so that they never again disobeyed his orders.' There were also successful campaigns against the Danes and the Huns.

Each spring the Franks held an assembly of all the soldiers, called a Marchfield. Here laws were passed and an army formed to fight during the summer months. From these gatherings Charlemagne led his troops not only into Germany, but also south to Italy and Spain.

In Spain he continued the work of his grandfather and father. In 777 he drove the Moslems back to the River Ebro. When his army was returning through the Pyrenees, the rearguard was attacked in the pass of Roncesvalles by the Basques, the people of south-western Gaul. The whole section was wiped out, in spite of a heroic defence by its leader Roland. (Many songs and poems were later written about him.) 'What is more,' wrote Einhard, 'this assault could not be avenged there and then, for the enemy scattered so quickly that no one knew where to find them.' Eventually, however, Charlemagne managed to capture the whole area up to the Ebro and then fortified the province against the Moslems.

It is clear, from reading about these conquests, that Charlemagne was an energetic and powerful king. Yet Einhard sometimes tried to show him to be greater than he was. Einhard stated that 'he so influenced the kings of the Irish that . . . they called themselves his slaves and subjects'. We know, however, that in England King Offa of Mercia refused to accept Charlemagne's superiority. Einhard also argued that Charlemagne was on such good terms with Haroun al-Raschid, the king of Persia, that 'Haroun valued his goodwill more than that of all the other kings in the world'. Yet when Charlemagne's ambassadors visited Persia, Haroun's official records did not even mention the fact.

Haroun-al-Raschid's envoys visit Charlemagne

Perhaps Charlemagne's greatest achievement was that he could govern this huge empire himself. He was constantly in the saddle, visiting the various tribes to defeat rebels, issue laws and settle quarrels. If a problem arose in an area he could not visit, he sent two important men as his representatives. They were called *missi dominici*, or the king's ambassadors. Charlemagne made them promise that 'in all cases, everywhere, in accordance with the will of God, they will administer the law justly to all people, rich and poor'. In addition each district had its own count. He was a royal official who collected taxes, punished criminals and called together a local army when it was needed. But it was only Charlemagne's power that made the *missi* and counts do their jobs properly.

The Coronation of 800

A fourteenth-century French manuscript shows Charlemagne's coronation at Rome

Charlemagne was also determined to continue his father's work in Italy. The new Lombard king, Desiderius, had taken some land from the pope, and recaptured some important cities. Charlemagne, therefore, went to Italy in 774 and besieged Desiderius in Pavia. Eventually the city surrendered. To prevent any further rebellion Charlemagne deposed Desiderius and made himself 'King of the Lombards'. As king he kept most of northern Italy for himself, but he did confirm the pope's right to certain lands in central Italy.

It was twenty years before Italy became a problem again. In 795 a new pope, Leo III, was chosen, but he was very unpopular with many people in Rome. Riots broke out in the city. Leo was accused of a number of crimes and fled in terror to Charlemagne. Einhard claimed that 'the people of Rome attacked him, put out his eyes and cut off his tongue'. Charlemagne went to Italy in the following year to punish the offenders. He was then crowned Roman Emperor in St Peter's Church on Christmas Day, AD 800.

There had been no emperor in Rome since the time of the barbarian invasions; yet here was Charlemagne, a barbarian himself, the new emperor.

Schools and learning

Following the barbarian invasions buildings were ruined, writing and sculpture stopped. Charlemagne realised that his people were ignorant. They could not read even the Bible and there were not enough schools. He himself was very interested in learning. Einhard wrote:

In all subjects he was taught by Alcuin, a man of the Saxon race who came from Britain and was the most learned man to be found anywhere. Under him the Emperor spent much time and effort studying. He applied himself to mathematics . . . and also tried to learn to write. With this object in view he used to keep writing tablets and notebooks under the pillow on his bed so that he could try his hand at forming letters during his leisure moments. But, although he tried very hard, he had begun too late in life and he made little progress.

The cathedral church at Aachen

Alcuin set up a school in Charlemagne's palace at Aachen and invited scholars from all over Europe. The sons of noblemen and courtiers learnt to read and write, and the scholars wrote textbooks to help them. In addition, Charlemagne sent a letter to each cathedral and monastery. They were commanded to 'teach those who by the gift of God are able to learn . . . so that children of slaves and the sons of free men may learn to read'. This command was not always obeyed, but some monasteries did develop good libraries. Manuscripts were kept and copied out in a new style of handwriting which was clear and easy to read. As a result of the work of the monks in these libraries, many works of ancient Roman writers were preserved for us to read today.

Other arts flourished too. For the first time music began to be written down, not just sung or played from memory. Sculpture and carving spread in churches, and manuscripts were beautifully decorated by the monks who copied them out. Charlemagne was also eager to revive the Roman ways of building. His palace at Aachen is typical of Roman style. Einhard wrote that:

He set in hand many projects which aimed at making his kingdom more attractive. . . . Outstanding among these are the great church at Aachen and the bridge over the River Rhine at Mainz which is 150 metres long. . . . In addition he commanded all bishops and priests to restore any church buildings which had fallen into ruin.

The first page of a book written in Latin in the year AD 800. It shows the new, clear, minuscule style of handwriting.

Whether the bishops obeyed or not, Charlemagne's care for his empire is obvious.

The death of Charlemagne

He then developed a pain in his side and a high temperature. He continued his dieting . . . but on the seventh day after taking to his bed he received holy communion and then he died.

CREATA SUNT ☩ DIGNUS

MICHAEL · S·MARIA · MATER DEI · SIOANNES BAPT

STABILI FUNDAMINE TEMPLUM QUOD CAROLUS PRINCEPS CONDIDIT ESSE VELIT

Charlemagne was buried in 814 in the cathedral which he himself had built at Aachen. Above his tomb this epitaph was written:

Beneath this stone lies the body of Charles the Great, the Christian Emperor, who greatly expanded the kingdom of the Franks, and reigned successfully for forty-seven years. He died when more than seventy years old.

Charlemagne was succeeded by his only son Louis, who was called 'the Pious'. Notker said that 'he was never weary of giving food and clothing to the poor'. However, Louis was too concerned with charity. He did not have the courage and determination to be a great ruler. Charlemagne's empire was huge and it needed constant patrolling: riots and rebellions were common.

Therefore when Louis died in 840, it was realised that the empire was too large for one man. As was common among the Franks, it was divided among Louis's three sons. By the partition of Verdun in 843 the eldest, Lothar, received the 'Middle Kingdom' and kept the title of Emperor. Charles 'the Bald' was given the kingdom of the West Franks, and Louis 'the German' received that of the East Franks.

Above King Louis the Pious

Left A drawing of King Charles the Bald from his prayer book

They could not, however, prevent the collapse of Charlemagne's empire. The Vikings, Moslems and Hungarians began their raids, and people looked for protection not to a distant king or emperor, but to a local lord. Charlemagne's last descendant died in 987 and by that time the Saxons had taken control of the kingdom of the East Franks and a new dynasty, the House of Capet, had taken over the kingdom of the West Franks. Medieval Germany and France had begun to appear.

768	Charlemagne king of the Franks	814	Death of Charlemagne
777	Defeat at Roncesvalles	840	Death of Louis the Pious
800	Charlemagne's coronation in Rome	843	Partition of Verdun

The interior of Aachen cathedral

Using the evidence: the conversion of the Saxons

It took Charlemagne many years of war to defeat and subdue the Saxons. This account comes from Einhard:

(1) The Saxons, like almost all the peoples living in Germany, were ferocious by nature. They were hostile to Christianity and they worshipped devils. They thought it no dishonour to break the laws, and hardly a day passed without some incident which was calculated to break the peace. The frontier between Frankish and Saxon Territory was flat and open country and the Saxons were constantly making raids for murder, plunder and arson.

A Saxon raid

As a result the Franks declared war on the Saxons. The war lasted for thirty-three long years and with great hatred on both sides, but the Saxons lost more men and battles than the Franks. The war would have been finished much quicker, had it not been for the faithlessness of the Saxons. On occasions they were totally defeated and promised to become Christians and send hostages to Charlemagne; but then they broke the promises they made. . . .

In the end, when all those who had been offering resistance had been utterly defeated, Charlemagne transported about 10 000 Saxon men, with their wives and children, and scattered them in very small groups throughout Gaul and Germany. At last the Saxons became Christians and joined the Franks . . . so much so, in fact, that during Charlemagne's wars against the Slavs some Saxons followed his standard, although their loyalty was feigned and not sincere.

Charlemagne was determined to stamp out revolt. On one occasion, after a Saxon rebellion, he is supposed to have massacred 45 000 Saxon prisoners who were being held in a church. There is also this story told by Notker the Stammerer:

(2) Once some barbarous peoples who came from the North ravaged a great part of Eastern Frankland. When this was reported to Charlemagne, he defeated them himself and ordered all their young men and children to be put in a line. He then took out his great sword and measured their height. All those who were taller than the sword were shortened by a head.

This grim tale shows how ruthless Charlemagne was. He was also ruthless in the peace terms he imposed on the Saxons, who were forced to become Christians:

(3) If any one of the race of the Saxons shall have wished not to be baptised but to remain a pagan, let him be punished by death.

If anyone conspires or plots with pagans against the Christians, let him be punished by death. . . .

We also command that all Saxons shall give a tithe [one-tenth] of their property and labour to the Churches and priests, so that the Church may receive one-tenth of all that every man earns.

Not everyone agreed with Charlemagne's policy. Alcuin, the learned monk who was head of Charlemagne's palace school, wrote this letter to the king:

(4) We know that the collection of tithes is a very good thing, but surely it is better not to insist on it too early and so ruin the true Christian faith of the Saxons. . . . It is much more important to give careful consideration to preaching and the proper observation of Church services among the Saxons . . . the miserable race of Saxons have been baptised, but have never really believed in Christ in their hearts. You cannot force a man to believe, and the exaction of the full burden of tithes from every household merely encourages the Saxons to rebel.

Questions and further work

1 Why is Einhard a good source of information about Charlemagne and his reign?
2 Give three pieces of evidence that Einhard admired Charlemagne.
3 Why do we need to be careful when reading Einhard's account? Would everyone have agreed that his description of the Emperor was a fair one (see page 47)?
4 Read again Document 1 where Einhard describes the Saxons. Does he show much sympathy for them? Write out three sentences which seem to be opinion rather than fact.
5 How might a Saxon describe the Franks? Write a short paragraph describing Charlemagne's achievements from a Saxon point of view.
6 Read Documents 1–4 again carefully. What was Charlemagne's way of dealing with the Saxons? Why did he act in this way? What was Alcuin's way? Which way do you think was the more sensible?
7 Imagine you were a Frankish count at the Marchfield of 777. Describe what happened during the visit to, and the return from, Spain.

A statue of Charlemagne

5 The Vikings

A Viking adventure

In 982, in Iceland, there was a bloody and violent quarrel between two Vikings. Why they fought we do not know. The story goes that in the quarrel one of them died. A trial was held. The other, Erik the Red, was found guilty of murder and banished from Iceland for three years.

Erik was put out to sea in a small boat with one or two friends. They sailed west. They stayed alive by hunting and fishing and eventually reached the coast of Greenland. For three years they sailed around its coast, making surveys of good harbours and farming land.

His exile over, Erik returned to Iceland. Here the people were poor and hungry. 'Men ate ravens and foxes and many loathsome things which they should not eat.' Erik told them of a rich green land (hence the name) to the west. Eleven shiploads of settlers and their cattle followed Erik to start a new home.

Two large settlements were founded on the coast of Greenland, and most men lived by rearing sheep and cattle.

Later in the same year, 986, a man called Bjarni sailed from Iceland to Greenland. In thick fog his ship drifted helplessly for days to the south west. When the fog lifted they sighted land but Bjarni did not wish to go ashore. Instead, he sailed north east until he reached Greenland.

This wooden Viking ship was reconstructed from one found in a burial mound at Gokstad in Norway. It was in such ships that men like Erik and Bjarni sailed.

The Gokstad ship preserved in a museum in Oslo

Did he see the coast of North America? Seventeen years later Leif Erikson, a son of Erik the Red, sailed to the south west from Greenland. He travelled hundreds of kilometres past Helluland and Markland until he came to a warmer area where salmon was caught and vines grew. This he named Vinland or Wineland. Two years later his brother, Thorvald, sailed to Vinland and stayed there for two years. When he was killed in an Indian raid, his followers returned to Greenland. One further expedition followed but then Viking exploration of North America came to an end.

The stories of these men come from sagas, songs which were sung around Viking camp-fires and written down about two or three hundred years after the voyages.

Who were the Vikings?

Adventurous sailors like Bjarni and Leif came originally from Norway, Sweden and Denmark (Scandinavia). The Vikings are usually remembered as seafarers and raiders but in their homeland they were peaceful farmers and fishermen.

Families were usually large and closely-knit, the whole family often living in one large house. This was generally built of wood, but the Vikings used stone where this was available. The cattle were kept separately in a byre or shed nearby. Most family houses had just one long room with a huge fire in the middle. In the evenings everyone would gather around it to eat and talk and then go to sleep.

The young Viking soon learned how to look after the herds from the older members of the family. He might make tools and help to build

A Viking warrior

An aerial photograph of a Viking settlement at Trelleborg in Denmark. Describe the position and shape of the long houses.

houses too. At the age of fourteen or fifteen he would go on his first voyage, often to England or Ireland, either to trade with or steal from the inhabitants. These young men lived at close quarters with their companions on board ship for weeks at a time. Sharing adventure, hardship and danger, they often became firm friends for life.

A carved Viking wagon, found at Oseberg in Norway

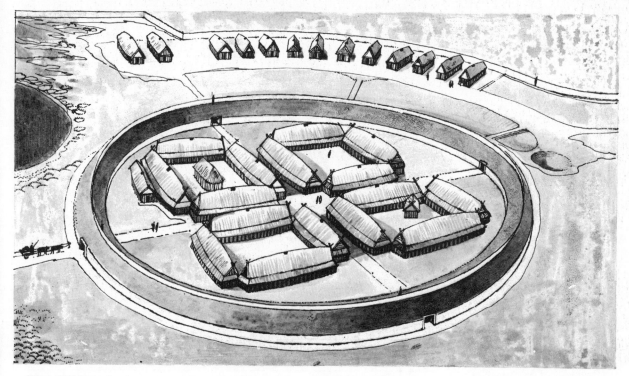

The Vikings had many gods to protect them. Odin, who brought them success in wars, and Frey, who made sure that the crops grew well, were just two. These and other gods were usually worshipped in huge log temples. The Vikings believed that when they died they went to Valhalla or heaven, a land of feasting and pleasure. Preparations for this life after death were taken very seriously:

When a great man among them dies, they make a grave like a large house and place him in it. With him they lay his clothes and also food, drink and money. They also lay his wife in the grave with him while she is still alive. Then the door of the grave is blocked up and she dies inside.

Sometimes the body of a warrior was laid in his ship with all his possessions. The ship was then buried under a mound or set on fire and allowed to drift away to sea.

Raiders and settlers

During the reign of Charlemagne, the Vikings began to sail from Scandinavia to raid nearby lands. Because of the harsh climate, the barren soil and a rise in population, they found it increasingly difficult to make a living from farming. When they put out from their harbours, their ships were a splendid sight:

One day we saw a ship ornamented all over with gold above the waterline and with fine dragon heads and a sail of rich cloth, most splendidly woven. Everybody wondered at the sight of it. The ship was painted in red and purple and gold and the dragon heads shone like gold in the sun.

A reconstruction of a Viking settlement in Denmark

A carved figurehead, found at Oseberg

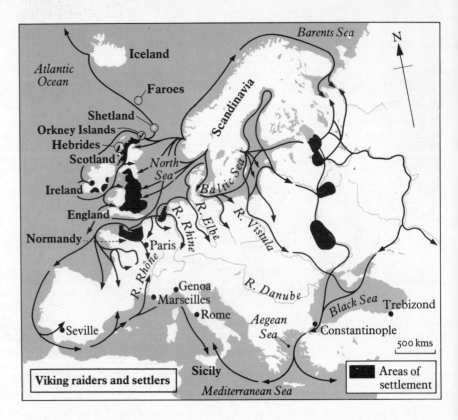

Map: Viking raiders and settlers. Labels include: Barents Sea, N, Iceland, Atlantic Ocean, Faroes, Shetland, Orkney Islands, Hebrides, Scotland, North Sea, Ireland, England, Normandy, Scandinavia, Baltic Sea, R. Elbe, R. Rhine, R. Vistula, Paris, R. Rhône, R. Danube, Genoa, Marseilles, Rome, Aegean Sea, Black Sea, Trebizond, Constantinople, Seville, Sicily, Mediterranean Sea, 500 kms, Areas of settlement, Viking raiders and settlers

Where did the Vikings sail to? The Swedes went eastwards to trade with the people of central Europe in what is now Russia. Some warriors even reached Constantinople and joined the emperor's bodyguard there. The Danes usually turned southwards. Sailing close to the coast and up the rivers, they looted and burned towns like Paris (845) as they went. Some even crossed the Bay of Biscay and in 862 entered the Mediterranean.

The Norwegians were probably the most adventurous seamen. They sailed far from land, guided by the sun and the stars. If they were caught in a fog they waited until it lifted and then corrected their course. At this time other Europeans were afraid to sail out of sight of land.

They began to settle in the Scottish isles and Ireland. Raids were made on lonely English monasteries. Lindisfarne suffered in 793 and Iona in 795. Between 900 and 950 the Norwegians formed large colonies in the seaports of Ireland, the Isle of Man and north west England. From these bases they sailed north and west to Iceland and then to Greenland and perhaps North America. One explorer returned from Iceland to Norway and said that 'butter dripped from every blade of grass in the land they had found'. No wonder there was soon a colony of about 20 000 Norwegians there.

Their raids struck terror into the people of Europe. Sailing up rivers and using horses captured from local villages, they made quick raids inland. Nowhere were towns or monasteries safe from attack. No wonder men prayed to God: 'From the terror of the Northmen, good

Carved silver goblets

Lord, deliver us.' This is a typical entry in the *Anglo-Saxon Chronicle*:

841. In this year Herebert was killed by heathen men and many others with him; and in the same year many men in Lincolnshire, East Anglia and Kent were killed by the enemy.

How do we know?

Our knowledge of the Vikings is limited. We know nothing, for instance, of the many ships which must have sailed the North Sea and the Atlantic Ocean and been lost in storms. We learn something from the remains of houses, barns and other buildings found by archaeologists in Scandinavia, Iceland and other places. Most exciting are the number of magnificent burial ships which have been dug up. These have told archaeologists a great deal, not only about Viking ships but also about the possessions and way of life of kings and nobles.

But the written evidence is not very good. English monks described in detail many Viking raids on monasteries. Understandably, however, they were very hostile to the Vikings and we cannot believe all that they wrote. Alcuin, at the court of Charlemagne, described the destruction of Lindisfarne (in 793) in a letter:

The heathens poured out the blood of saints around the altar, and trampled on the bodies of saints in the temple of God, like dung in the streets.

We are left in no doubt as to Alcuin's opinion of the Vikings, but he tells us little about them.

The Vikings' own sagas are not reliable either. The stories were handed down by word of mouth and became exaggerated and distorted in the telling. Much detailed information was lost in this way.

The Danes

Danish attacks on England began in the year 835. The first raid was on the areas around the mouth of the River Thames, but soon the whole of the south of England was under attack. The *Anglo-Saxon Chronicle* records that the Danes were usually, but not always, victorious:

851. [The Danes] stormed Canterbury and London and routed the King of the Mercians with his army and went south across the Thames. King Ethelwulf with the army of the West Saxons fought against them and there inflicted on them the greatest slaughter we have ever heard of, and had the victory there.

This battle took place near Basingstoke in Hampshire. The Danes were undismayed by their defeat and a huge new army arrived in England in 865. Marching north they captured Nottingham and York. King Edmund of East Anglia was killed in battle and the Danes gained control of large areas of land.

The wealthy kingdom of Wessex was a prize the Danes were eager to capture. A series of fierce battles was fought. The last of these was at Ashdown, near Reading, where King Ethelred of Wessex and his younger brother, Alfred, finally defeated them. This was in 871, but only three months after the battle Ethelred died, perhaps from the wounds he had received.

Alfred was proclaimed king, but soon faced further trouble from the Danes. In 876 Guthrum and a fresh army invaded Wessex. They captured the town of Wareham and then rode quickly to take the fortress of Exeter. Alfred had to pay them tribute to leave. The following year, though, they came again and attacked Alfred's court while it was peacefully celebrating Christmas at Chippenham. Alfred hastily fled to the Isle of Athelney, relatively safe because it was surrounded by marshland. There he is supposed to have been given the task of watching the cakes in the oven and to have allowed them to burn.

The Viking leader Guthrum with his uncle King Harold Fairhair

From Athelney, however, he was constantly sending out scouts for news and after Easter was able to lead the men of Wessex against the Danes again. This time Alfred won a decisive victory at Edington in Wiltshire and peace was made. Guthrum was baptised a Christian and gave hostages to show that he would keep his word. He promised to remain in East Anglia and Lincolnshire and not to attack the men of Wessex.

This new Danish kingdom was called the Danelaw. Here Guthrum's men settled down as farmers with their own laws and customs. They even kept their promise not to raid Wessex and treated the Saxon people who still lived in eastern England fairly. Many places in these counties have Danish names to this day. Examples are names ending in -*ly* or -*thorpe*, meaning a village, or names ending in -*toft*, meaning a farmhouse.

King Alfred the Great

Alfred's reign lasted another twenty years after the battle of Edington. He called all the nobles of Wessex to a meeting and they made a list of good laws which everyone should keep. They also drew up a list of fines to be paid by any man who broke these laws. The most serious crime was treason with a severe penalty: 'If anyone plots against the king's life, he should pay with his own life and all that he has.'

Alfred was aware that the Danes might return. He therefore built great warships, said to be twice as big as those of his enemy. He tried to improve his army by allowing half his men to fight while the other half remained at work in the fields; this reduced the usual mass-desertions at harvest time. Alfred built many forts or 'bųrhs', especially near or around big towns. Ditches were dug and the earth was piled high. On top of this pile a wooden stockade was built.

It was a good job that Alfred took these precautions. The Danes did return in 892, and for four years there was fighting which ended in defeat for the invading army.

Like Charlemagne, Alfred was interested in learning and teaching. Bishop Asser taught him to read and later wrote a biography of him. Alfred tried to persuade his nobles to learn to read and invited educated men to his court. They translated into Saxon many Latin books like Bede's *History*, and it was at this time that a new history of the deeds of the Saxons was begun. This was the *Anglo-Saxon Chronicle* (see page

15). On one occasion Alfred was visited by a sailor from the far north called Othere. Alfred wrote down this man's tale in his own book:

Othere dwelt in the far north. Once upon a time he desired to see how far north his country extended and whether anyone lived in the waste. So he sailed due north for three days along the coast. Then he was as far north as any whale-hunter had been. Then he carried on for another three days and then turned east for a further four days. . . . By this time he had found horse-whales, so

The Fuller brooch shows the five senses. It was made of silver, probably during Alfred's reign.

called because of their fine teeth, and he gave Alfred some of these teeth. He said he had killed sixty in two days.

Whether Alfred believed Othere's story or not, he was always keen to learn new things.

'Kings of All Britain'

After Alfred died in 899, his successors gradually conquered the whole of England, including the Danelaw. They protected their conquests with many new burhs. Less than fifty years after Alfred's death, his grandson, Athelstan, was calling himself 'King of all Britain' on his coins. The country was then split up into shires, like modern counties, and hundreds, a smaller area consisting of one hundred households.

One of Athelstan's successors was Ethelred 'the Unready'. When the Danish raids began again he had to pay them money (Danegeld) to leave, because he was too weak to fight them. In 1016 his son, Edmund Ironside, was defeated by Cnut, a Danish king, who thus became king of England. He and his two sons reigned until 1042. Cnut, at least, ruled fairly and wisely, keeping Alfred's laws and building many churches and monasteries.

793	Vikings raided Lindisfarne
835	First Danish raid on England
845	Danes attacked Paris
871	Alfred's victory at Ashdown
879	Alfred's victory at Edington
886	Peace between Alfred and Guthrum
899	Death of Alfred
982	Erik the Red sailed to Greenland
986	Bjarni set sail (and sighted North America?)
1003	Leif Erikson's voyage (to North America?)
1016	Cnut king of England

Left A page from a medieval manuscript at Winchester. It shows King Canute and his wife Queen Emma of Normandy. They are putting a cross on the altar of the minster at Winchester. One monk wrote of Canute, 'Whenever he went into any church, he was received with great honour'.

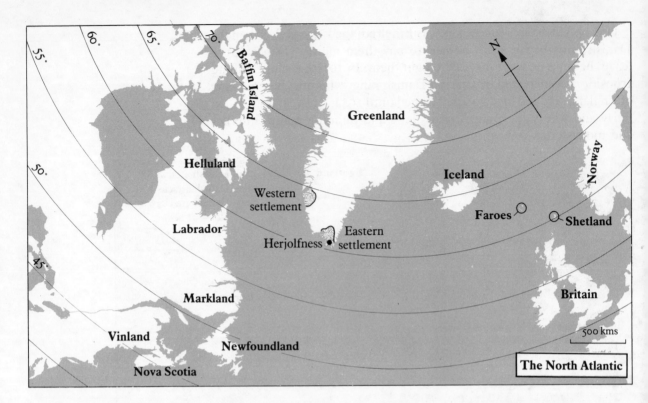

The North Atlantic

Using the evidence: the Vikings and Vinland

We cannot say for certain whether Bjarni or Leif Erikson or any other Viking adventurer saw or set foot in the North American continent. There are four main sources of evidence but none is totally reliable.

The *Saga of the Greenlanders* was written in the twelfth century, nearly two hundred years after the events it describes. It tells how Bjarni and his followers set out from Iceland to Greenland in 986:

(1) When they were ready, they set out. They sailed for three days, until they lost sight of land. Then the wind eased, and a north wind set in, bringing fog. They had no idea where they were, and this went on for several days. At last the sun appeared, and they were able to distinguish the quarters of the sky. So they hoisted sail again, and sailed on for a night and a day, and then they sighted land.

They discussed what land this could be, and Bjarni said he did not think it was Greenland. When they asked if they should put in nearer land, he told them to sail close in. This they did, and soon saw that there were no mountains, only low hills covered with forest. So they sailed on, leaving the land on their port side.

They sailed for two days before they sighted land again. They asked Bjarni if this might be Greenland, but he said this was no more Greenland than the first place they had sighted, 'for in Greenland, they say, there are high mountains covered with snow'. They soon approached this land, and saw that it was flat and covered with forest. The wind dropped, and the men thought it would be best to make for land, but Bjarni would not agree. They said they needed water and wood, but Bjarni said they did not. The crew grumbled about this, but he ordered them to hoist sail, which they did. Then they sailed out to sea again, and for three days ran before a south-westerly wind.

Then they saw a third land, high and mountainous. They asked Bjarni if he would land here, but he refused. They sailed along the shore, and found that it was an island. Then they turned away from the land, and stood out to sea with the same wind; but a gale came on, and Bjarni ordered a reef to be taken in, and told them not to sail the ship harder than she would stand.

After three days and nights land was sighted for the fourth time, and when they asked him whether this was Greenland, Bjarni replied, 'This is most like what I have heard of Greenland. We will go ashore here.' In the evening they landed beside a cape, where they found a boat. On this cape lived Bjarni's father, Herjolf, and the place is called Herjolfsness.

About fifty years after the *Saga of the Greenlanders* was written, a second account appeared. This was the *Saga of Erik the Red*. In this account, Bjarni's voyage is not mentioned. Instead it describes how Leif Erikson tried to find the unknown lands to the west:

(2) Leif, son of Erik the Red, went to Bjarni, and bought his ship and got together a crew of thirty-five men. . . . Among the crew was a man from a southern country, called Tyrker.

The ship was made ready, and they put to sea. They came first to the land which Bjarni had discovered last. They sailed up to it, dropped anchor, put out a boat, and went ashore, but could see no grass. Inland there were high snowy mountains, and between the sea and the mountains nothing but rock, and they decided that this land was of little use.

But Leif said, 'We won't have it said of us that we did not go ashore, as they

said of Bjarni, for I shall give this land a name, and I call it Helluland [land of rocks].'

Then they went back on board, sailed away and found another land, and sailed near in, and dropped anchor, and put out a boat and landed. Here it was flat and covered with trees, and the beach was low, with white sand everywhere. Then Leif said, 'This land shall have a name to suit its appearance. We will call it Markland [land of forests].'

Then they hurried aboard and sailed away. There was a gale blowing from the north east and it was two days before they saw land again. They sailed towards it, and saw it was an island lying to the north of the mainland. There they landed in fine weather. There was dew on the grass, and they touched it with their fingers and tasted it, and they had never tasted anything so sweet as this dew.

Then they went on board and sailed into the channel that ran between the island and a cape jutting out northward from the land, and sailed on westwards past the cape. But there the water was very shallow, and their ship ran aground, and at low tide it was a long way from the water to their ship. But they were so keen to get ashore that they would not wait for the tide, but ran to the shore, and came to a place where a small river flowed out of a lake.

As soon as their ship was afloat again, they took the boats and towed the ship up the river and into the lake, and there they anchored, carried their things ashore, and set up their tents. They decided to settle there for the winter, and built a big house. There was no shortage of salmon, either in the river or the lake, and they were the biggest salmon they had ever seen. The land appeared to be so rich that there was no need to gather fodder for the cattle for the winter. There was no frost during the winter, and the grass did not wither very much. Day and night were more equally divided than in Iceland or Greenland. . . .

When spring came, they packed up and sailed for home. Leif named the land after its fruits, and called it Wineland.

It is difficult to work out whether either of these two men, Bjarni or Leif, actually saw the North American coast. Was Helluland really Baffin Island or Markland really Labrador?

The third piece of evidence, the account in the so-called Vinland Map, was written in the fifteenth century, just before the voyages of Christopher Columbus.

(3) By God's will, after a long voyage from the island of Greenland to the South towards the most distant remaining parts of the Western ocean sea, sailing Southwards amidst the ice, the companions Bjarni and Leif Erikson discovered a new land, extremely fertile and having vines, the which land they named Vinland.

The fourth piece of evidence we have concerns archaeology. Historians have long looked for physical remains of Vikings in the North American coast and a number of fakes have appeared. Recently, however, two things have been discovered in Greenland. Archaeologists have found a Red Indian arrow-head made of Labrador quartzite stone in a Viking churchyard in western Greenland. In addition, several Viking coffins have been found made from larchwood. Larch was unknown in Scandinavia or Greenland, but it was and still is common in Labrador. Do these finds indicate that Vikings brought these objects back from North America? Archaeologists have also recently found in

The map shows various place names including:

Iotun heimax.
Rifeland   Narve öe   D   E   F   Biar maland
MARE GLACIALE.   Norvegia
GRONLANDIA   Huudferk
Ifland
Ferœ
Frisland   Hetland
H
Helleland   G
Orcades
SIUR di Stephanii terrarum hyperborearu delineatio Año 1570
Markland   Winlandie
IR LAND   BRITANNIA
Skraelinge Land.   Promontorium Winlandiæ
A
B

The Vinland Map is now kept in the royal library at Copenhagen

Newfoundland the remains of a house very like a Viking one with scraps of worked iron and bronze nearby and a stone anvil. This is significant because neither the Red Indians nor the Eskimos were skilled in metal work at this time.

Questions and further work

1 From the description on page 65 draw a picture of a burh. List the other things King Alfred did to make sure that the Danes would not defeat him in battle.
2 If you look at the map of the North Atlantic on page 68 the accounts of the Viking voyages become clearer. Trace the map, then following Bjarni's account in Document 1, start at the end of his voyage and mark his route backwards from Herjolfsness. Using a different colour mark Leif Erikson's voyage on the same map.

(Also mark Iceland, Greenland, Herjolfsness, Markland, Helluland and Vinland.) How closely did Leif follow Bjarni's route?

3 List the concrete evidence, firstly in Bjarni's story, and secondly in Leif's story, which helps us to understand where they were.

4 Imagine you are one of Bjarni's crew in 986. Write a diary account of the voyage and your feelings about it.

5 From the evidence available in the documents is it probable the Vikings discovered North America? List the evidence to support your answer.

The powers of Europe

6 The Normans

The Dukes of Normandy

The map shows the duchy of Normandy in northern France. In the ninth century this area had been raided many times by the Vikings. It was attacked once again in 911, by a Norwegian pirate called Rolf the Ganger. Rolf probably received this name because he was so big that no horse could carry him and he had to 'gang afoot'. After a life of thieving and pillaging he had been exiled by King Harold of Norway. He then took his many Viking followers to raid the coast of northern France. The Frankish king at Paris, Charles the Simple, was afraid to fight the powerful Norwegian, and to prevent bloodshed he gave him the duchy of Normandy.

In 911 the two leaders met. Rolf swore on oath to be loyal to the king and not to raid his lands. In such ceremonies of homage it was customary for the duke to kneel before the king or kiss his feet. Duke Rolf was too proud a Viking to do this, so he asked one of his companions to do it for him. The man knelt down and raised the king's foot, but, to the delight of the Vikings, he lifted it too high and the king fell flat on his back. (Had Rolf and his friend planned the whole thing?)

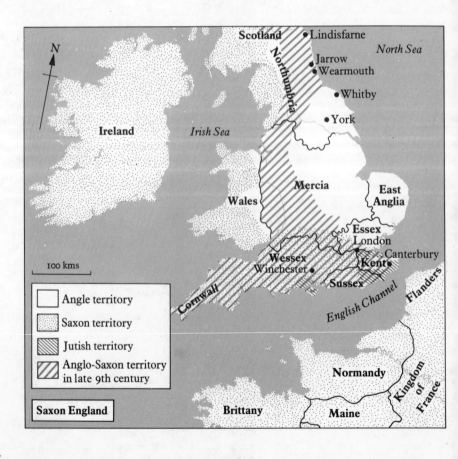

Saxon England

- Angle territory
- Saxon territory
- Jutish territory
- Anglo-Saxon territory in late 9th century

100 kms

Like their Viking ancestors the Normans were a powerful and able race. They were ruthless and ambitious. One Italian chronicler wrote:

> They delight in arms and horses, the luxuries of dress, the exercises of hunting and hawking; but in battle they can endure any harsh climate with effort and determination.

These qualities enabled Rolf and his successors to make Normandy one of the most powerful states in Europe. In 1035 Duke Robert the Magnificent was killed while returning from a pilgrimage to Jerusalem. His illegitimate son William became the new duke.

William was a typical Norman. In 1046 a group of rebel barons plotted to capture and murder him. He decisively crushed them in the following year at the battle of Val és Dunes:

> Hurling himself upon his enemies, William terrified them with slaughter. Some were killed in the battle, crushed or trampled upon by those who fled. Many of the horsemen with their mounts were drowned in the River Orne.

William won two more great victories in 1054 and 1057 at Mortemer and Varaville, both against his overlord, Henry I, the king of France. After Henry died in 1060 William's power was even greater and he added to it by acquiring the neighbouring territory of Maine in 1063.

William and the English throne

England, meanwhile, was ruled by Edward the Confessor, a Saxon who had been brought up with William in Normandy. He was a pious man who lacked the ruthlessness and determination of William. After 1053 he was virtually under the control of Harold Godwinson, the powerful Earl of Wessex. Edward died on 6 January 1066 with no child to succeed him.

On his death bed he is thought to have named Earl Harold as his successor. Whether he did or not, Harold was immediately accepted by the other barons in the Witan, or Council, and crowned by Archbishop Stigand of Canterbury at Westminster Abbey. Harold had a strong

Left King Edward on his deathbed

Below The Bayeux Tapestry: King Harold is crowned by Archbishop Stigand

claim to the throne since Edward had married Harold's sister Edith and Harold had often led the king's army against the Welsh. After his coronation he toured the country, forcing his new subjects to recognise him as king.

Unfortunately for Harold two other men also wanted the crown at this time: Harald Hardrada, king of Norway, and William, the Norman duke. The Norwegian's claim to the throne was not very strong, but he was a descendant of Cnut, the Danish king of England (1016–39). William of Normandy, on the other hand, had known Edward in his childhood and had probably visited England in 1051. Edward may even have promised him the crown.

More important, in 1063 or 1064 Harold of Wessex was shipwrecked off the coast of France. This account of what happened comes from a Norman chronicler:

Harold was conducted with great ceremony to Rouen. There the Duke rejoiced to have so famous a guest, a man who in England was second only to the king. ... When they met, Harold swore loyalty to the Duke on ancient relics, and took an oath, of his own free will, that he would use all his influence to ensure that after the death of the king the kingdom of England would be the property of the Duke.

The Bayeux Tapestry: What is happening in this picture?

The same picture is shown in the Bayeux Tapestry. Thus when Harold accepted the crown in 1066, he was breaking his oath, a very serious offence in the Middle Ages. Why do you think the Norman chronicler emphasised that Harold took the oath 'of his own free will'?

1066

Supported by Pope Alexander II, William assembled a huge army at St Valéry. Throughout July and August Harold had waited near the Isle of Wight for William's army to land. Many of his men tired of waiting and, because Harold could not feed them, went home.

On 8 September Harold heard of the arrival of the Norwegian army at

The motte and bailey castle at Pleshey

Tynemouth. By 25 September he had marched north and defeated them at the battle of Stamford Bridge. But his triumph was short-lived. Two days later he learned that William's army, previously delayed by contrary winds, had landed at Pevensey.

He immediately set off for Kent. Though many of his men had died at Stamford Bridge and others deserted on the way south, he bravely insisted on going to face William. When he set up his position above the Normans at Hastings he may have had just two thousand professional soldiers (his huscarls), and perhaps three thousand peasants armed with pitchforks and stones. The Normans, on the other hand, had about seven thousand well-armed and experienced troops, mostly mounted knights, archers and foot soldiers.

William's victory at Hastings was complete. Many of the thegns or nobles of Saxon England were killed along with Harold. The Conqueror marched through Kent, around the south side of London, took Winchester and then turned back east to capture London. On Christmas Day he was crowned king of England in Westminster Abbey by Archbishop Ealdred of York.

William's rule in England (1066–87)

In 1067 William set out to conquer the Saxon people. He built a castle in London, on the site of his later famous White Tower, and confiscated the lands of all who had fought against him at Hastings. He easily put down rebellions, at Exeter in 1068 and in the north in 1069. Stone motte-and-bailey castles were constructed at Nottingham, Warwick and Lincoln and other strategic places. After the northern rebellion, he ravaged the county of Yorkshire 'with all the force he could muster'.

His aim was to prevent further risings.

Never before did William commit so much cruelty. He set no bounds to his fury, but ordered corn, cattle and every sort of food to be collected in heaps and set on fire. Innocent children, young men and old died of hunger.

It is significant that this criticism comes from a Norman!

William then crossed to Cheshire, defeated the Mercians and built castles at Chester and Stafford. Only one Saxon rebel remained and the *Anglo-Saxon Chronicle* recounts his revolt in Peterborough in 1070:

Forthwith, in the morning, the outlaws came with many ships and wanted to enter the monastery but the monks held them back. They eventually entered through the Bolhithe Gate, and the monks came towards them to ask for a truce; the rebels, however, ignored the monks, entered the monastery . . . and took the golden crown from our lord's head. They also plundered two golden shrines and nine of silver, together with fifteen great crucifixes of gold and silver. They said they did all this out of loyalty to the monastery. Then they sailed to Ely where they left the treasure. (1072) When William found out

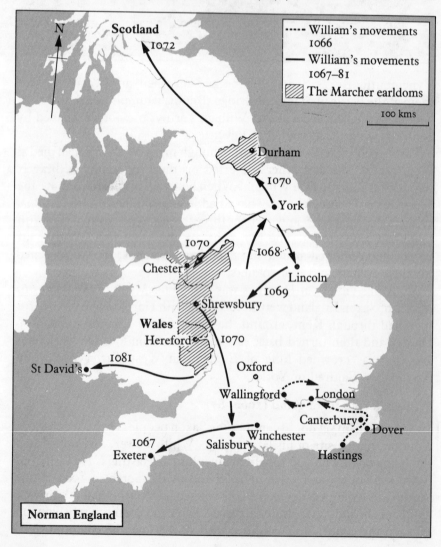

Norman England

about all this, he called out a naval force and an army and invaded that part of the country, so that the rebels all surrendered to him, with the exception of the valiant Hereward and those who escaped with him.

Hereward's final defeat was marked by the building of a motte-and-bailey castle at Ely.

William and his two sons William II (1087–1100) and Henry I (1100–35) made many changes in England. The Conqueror distributed the estates of the great Saxon earls among those followers who had helped him at Hastings. He also made a bargain with them. He would protect them if they served in his army for part of the year, with their knights. Each baron then kept part of the land he was given for himself and gave the rest to the knights who served him. They, in their turn, kept part of their land and gave the rest to their peasants, villeins and cottagers, who worked on the knights' land in return. Really little changed for these peasants, after the Conquest. They merely exchanged their Saxon lords for new Norman lords.

The two volumes of Domesday Book, resting on the iron chest in which they were kept at Westminster

The Domesday Book

We know about William's changes because in 1086 he ordered a complete survey of the country which became known as the Domesday Book. William sent royal officials around the country to ask certain questions about every manor: who held it; how much it was worth; how much it had been worth under Edward the Confessor, and so on. Many men thought the king was prying too closely into their business. One Saxon chronicler wrote:

So very thoroughly did William have the inquiry carried out that there was not a single piece of land, not even an ox, cow or pig which escaped the notice of the survey.

In eade villa hb Vichil. 1. maner de. uu. car. id gtd. ria. e ad. uu. car.

In Scinestorp Vlfi 7 Archil hbr. 11. aran de. 11. car. 7 v. boū ad gtd. tra e. ad. 11. car. Ic. e ibi in dnio .1. car. 7 u. bord. Hi vi. maner. T.R.E. uat vi. lib. m. uu. lib. Nigel hie de comite Robto.

h soca ptinet ad Wireha. Domecaftre. Benedlea. Langeroure. Adeuuic. Sandalia. Simul ad gtd. uu. car. Ic ibi in dnio. 1. car. 7i. foch. 7 vn. uilt 7 vui. bord. hmes v. car. Silua modica. vu. gk lg. 7 vui lat.
OSCOT CROS WAPENTAC

In Aderuic funt. 11. boū ad gtd. foca e in arera. Ibi hie Nigel ibi. 1. car. T.R.E. uat xl. fot. m. v. fot.
STAINCROS WAPENTAC

A short extract from a page of the Domesday Book. It deals with Lincolnshire. Can you identify any of the places mentioned?

The Tower of London, a stone keep, built by William the Conqueror

Here is a typical entry for Yorkshire; what can we learn from it? (What had happened in Yorkshire just after the Conquest to make the land 'waste'?)

In Shipley Ravenchil held three carucates of land in the reign of King Edward. There was room for two ploughs and it was worth ten shillings. Now it is waste. Ilbert de Lacy holds it.

The year after the survey, William died at Rouen. His achievement was recorded by a chronicler:

Among other things he made peace over the whole realm, so that an honest man could travel over the kingdom with his pockets full of gold, and no man dared strike another.

Ely Cathedral. This was rebuilt during William's reign and some parts of this picture date back to his time. Norman arches are long and narrow. The more decorated arches were added by later builders.

His sons added to this. William and Henry built many stone keeps like the one at Rochester. Norman–French became the official language at court. Many churches and seven new cathedrals were built using stone and the round Norman arches familiar to this day.

The Normans in Italy

Long before the reign of William the Conqueror, soldiers from Normandy had been going on pilgrimages to Jerusalem. They returned via Italy where they helped the local people in their wars against the Moslems. They were rewarded with luxuries, food, and even land. News of Italy's wealth soon spread to Normandy and men began to ride south in the spring to seek their fortunes. Such men were the twelve sons of Tancred d'Hauteville. One of them, Robert Guiscard, conquered Apulia, Calabria, and Bari, securing the whole of southern Italy. This was a feat equal to that of William the Conqueror. Robert, like William, became a very important ruler. He was a friend of the pope and rescued Gregory VII in 1084 when the latter was attacked in Rome by the Emperor Henry IV. He also raided many Greek cities and captured their treasure. It is not surprising that a chronicler described him as the 'Terror of the World'.

Norman cloisters in a church in Sicily

King Roger II of Sicily receiving his crown from Christ. A mosaic from Palermo.

After his death in 1085 his younger brother, Roger, continued his work. Roger fought for thirty years to capture Sicily from the Moslems and his son, Bohemund, captured the Principality of Antioch on the First Crusade. Under Roger II in the twelfth century the Norman kingdom of Sicily became a well-organised state. It was almost the only one in Europe at the time where Moslems, Jews and Christians were all tolerated.

Using the evidence: the Battle of Hastings

A cool autumn evening, 13 October 1066. Harold's army, bedraggled and tired from their long march south from Stamford Bridge, set up camp on Senlac Hill near Hastings. With pride they raised his standard, the Dragon of Wessex.

William's army was based at Pevensey, some twelve kilometres away. Later that night, Norman scouts rode into the duke's camp and told him of Harold's arrival. William gave his orders quickly. He had waited for this moment. That night his army spent much of their time in prayer.

At dawn next morning they were ready. This account was written by a Norman soldier in 1071. He was not present at the battle, but he later became William's chaplain:

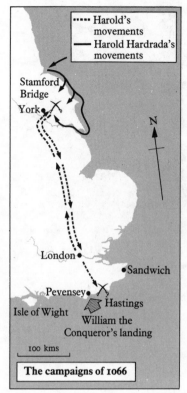

The campaigns of 1066

(1) William's army advanced steadily in good order. They carried the Pope's banner proudly at their head. In front William placed footsoldiers with crossbows and arrows; second came his heavily-armed infantry, clad in hauberks; finally came the squadrons of knights. In their midst, William sat proudly astride his horse, controlling the whole army.

Harold's army was a vast host, gathered from all the provinces of England and reinforced by their allies, the Danes. They did not dare to fight on equal terms, so they took up their position on a hill with a forest behind them. They dismounted and drew themselves up in close order on foot.

The story goes that a minstrel knight called Ivo asked a favour of William. He wanted to lead the first charge. Up the hill he drove his horse, followed by other knights. But the Saxon wall of infantry held firm and Ivo was slain.

The Norman soldier continues his story:

The Norman foot soldiers then attacked, in spite of the difficulty of the ground. They hurled spears and javelins at the English. The latter resisted bravely and returned the fire with spears, axes and stones. It seemed that our troops would be overwhelmed by the missiles.

Then our knights crashed into the enemy with their shields, anxious to use their swords at close quarters. The English remained on high ground and kept close order. They were also superior in numbers and in the way their spears broke our shields. Thus they pushed our knights down the hill.

At this point the Normans thought William had been killed. He was nowhere to be seen. Suddenly:

William stood boldly in front of those in flight. 'Look at me well; I am still alive.' He restored their courage and our knights turned to face the following English and cut them down. . . .

Heartened by their success our men marched up the hill a second time. They realised they would suffer heavy losses, but then remembered the trick of retreating. They turned round and pretended to flee. Several thousand English quickly gave pursuit. The Normans suddenly turned their horses, surrounded the enemy and cut them down. Twice this trick was employed with great success and at last the English tired under constant pressure.

It was quite late in the evening when the battle was finally won.

The second account of the battle, written much later by a Saxon monk, tells a very different story:

'Hic Haroldus Rex interfectus est'. This is Latin for 'Here King Harold is slain'. It was always thought that King Harold is the man with the arrow in his eye. Now, however, many scholars think he is the man killed by the sword. Notice the weapons and armour of the soldiers. What is happening in the border at the bottom of the picture?

(2) After the battle at Stamford Bridge, the King heard of Duke William's arrival with a huge army at Pevensey. He marched his army with all haste to London. He knew that many of his men had died at Stamford and that much of his army had not yet arrived. Yet he continued with all speed into Sussex to meet his enemy. On 22 October, before a third of his army had arrived, he joined battle with William. The English army had a very small space; and many soldiers, seeing the difficult position, deserted King Harold. Even so he fought bravely from dawn till dusk, and the enemy's army made little impression on him until, after a great slaughter on both sides, the King, alas, fell. Nearly all the barons of England died with him.

The English flee, with the Normans in hot pursuit

Questions and further work

1 The Saxon and Norman stories differ on many points. What do they tell us about each of the following:
   (a) the size of the English army;
   (b) the size of the Norman army;
   (c) the position of the Saxon army;
   (d) Harold's and William's parts in the battle;
   (e) why the Normans won the battle?

2 In what other ways do the two stories disagree? Why do you think they differ?

3 Make a list of any statements in Documents 1 and 2 that you think are false. Why do you think the writers included them? Which account do you think is the more reliable?

4 Imagine you are one of Harold's huscarls or bodyguard. Write a brief diary account of the events of August to October 1066.

5 Retell the story of the battle in your own words, including only those facts which you believe to be true.

The two archbishops

The meeting at Rheims 1049

On 1 October 1049, in the Cathedral of Rheims in France, a short tubby man, full of bustle and energy, conducted a meeting. Before him sat a good number of bishops. They had come from far and near for the occasion. There was even one from England.

The little man stood up and addressed them. He was the new pope Leo IX. He had come all the way from Rome especially to talk to them. He welcomed all those present. Then, to their horror, he asked each one to stand up in turn and say whether he had paid money for his post.

The first bishop stood up but said nothing. Others looked round in panic. They could not tell lies to the pope. One said his parents had paid money but he had been unaware of the fact. Another excused himself by saying that his father, who had been bishop before him, had paid for his son to succeed. Suddenly, one man got up and hurriedly left the cathedral. He was the bishop of Langres. Pope Leo IX deposed him from his office the next day.

The bishops

Bishops were leaders of the church in Europe. They were supposed to be men of God, holy men. However, some of them did not lead good lives, like Megingard, a German:

In every divine service he loved brevity. He preferred a long meal to a long service. There was one occasion when he was singing Mass on Easter Sunday. Other priests started to sing the lengthy parts of the service, but the bishop interrupted them: 'You fellows are mad. By singing for such a long time you are making me die of hunger and thirst.'

It was to remove such bishops that Pope Leo went to Rheims. Later, another pope, Gregory VII, also attacked the bishops. Gregory was very determined and, like Leo, full of energy. Many legends grew up about him. One told how one day Gregory went riding with Abbot Hugh of Cluny. The horses were walking rhythmically, slow and steady, the two men were lost in thought. Hugh was thinking what a proud and determined man Gregory was. Suddenly Gregory shouted: 'It's a lie! I seek not my own glory, only the good of the Church.'

On occasions, popes, like Leo and Gregory, quarrelled with kings over bishops. The kings thought bishops should obey them. The popes naturally disagreed. Pope Gregory quarrelled with the Emperor Henry IV, and only after a long and bitter dispute, did Henry give in at Canossa in Italy:

There, for three successive days, Henry stood in the snow before the castle, dressed in rough cloth and pitifully pleading for forgiveness.

King William Rufus and Archbishop Anselm in England

The scene was the royal castle of Rockingham in Northamptonshire, on a spring day in March 1095. At the castle were:

(1) King William II Rufus of England, the son of William the

Opposite This is a fresco or wall painting, from the church of Santa Maria Novella in Florence. At the top Christ is seated in triumph. Below him, St Peter (holding the keys of the Kingdom of Heaven) and other saints admit good Christians through the gates. At the bottom the pope and other churchmen are sitting with their congregations.

An Italian carving of St Anselm

Pope Urban II preaches in France

Conqueror, young, impatient, determined. Rufus had serious problems. His armies were being attacked in Scotland and Wales. There were rumours that some barons were plotting against him. And now, to cap it all, his Archbishop of Canterbury was opposing him.

(2) Archbishop Anselm of Canterbury, a saintly, scholarly man, old and tired. He had been named as archbishop by Rufus two years earlier.

(3) The English bishops. Most were appointed by the king and held land from him, but the Archbishop was their head.

(4) Many important barons, loyal servants of the king.

The story so far: in Rome two rivals each claimed to be the real pope. In 1093, before becoming Archbishop, Anselm had supported Pope Urban II. Now, he wanted to visit Rome to collect his *pallium*, a piece of white ermine fur, which showed he was archbishop.

The king objected. He had not decided who was the real pope. And he felt he, not Anselm, should decide for England. The quarrel became bitter. On one occasion, Rufus sent a messenger to Anselm:

Tell the Archbishop that I hated him yesterday, and hate him more today, and shall hate him even more tomorrow.

In March 1095 Anselm and Rufus met to try to reach an agreement.

The Council of Rockingham 1095

In his opening speech to the barons and bishops, Anselm said he wanted to be free to go to Pope Urban in Rome.

1 Why do you think he told his audience the following things?
  (a) He had not wished to be made archbishop: the king forced him into it.
  (b) He had given his support to Pope Urban before he became archbishop.
  (c) He had always 'dwelt in concord with all men'.

He then asked the bishops to give him their help. Should he go to Rome? Or should he obey the king and not go? The bishops looked uneasy. They started to talk among themselves. What should they say?

Anselm and the bishops at Rockingham

2 Imagine you are one of the bishops. Which of the following pieces of advice would you give? Bear in mind what it says about bishops at the beginning.
  (a) Anselm should obey the king. William Rufus is the lord of all men in England.
  (b) Anselm should go to Rome. The pope is head of the whole church.
  (c) Avoid giving a straight answer, because you are bound to offend someone if you do.

Here is the reply the bishops really gave:

We know you are wise and a lover of the good. For this reason you do not need our counsel in so deep a matter. If indeed you will refer the matter to our lord the King, we will watch over your interests as we should our own. Nonetheless, if you bid us do so, we will relate your words to our lord the King, and inform you of his opinion.

3 List in your own words what they actually said. Why do you think they said these things?

The bishops took Anselm's questions to the king.

4 Imagine you are the king. Which of the following three things would you do now, and why?

(a) Be furious with Anselm. Go straight to see him and tell him who is in charge.

(b) Take time to think the matter over carefully.

(c) Try to talk to the bishops to make sure they are on your side.

This is what Rufus actually did:

Because it was a Sunday, the king commanded that the whole question be postponed until tomorrow, and that Anselm should return to his lodging.

5 What do you think Rufus might have done in the meantime?

The Council was deadlocked. The two men would not compromise. The next day Anselm left the Council and within a year had gone into exile in France.

Seventy-five years later a more dramatic conflict occurred.

Anselm's seal

Using the evidence: Thomas Becket

The murder

This is the story of a murder. Imagine the altar steps of Canterbury Cathedral, lit by candlelight: in the background, the chanting monks, the smell of burning incense. There is peace, quiet, calm. Archbishop Thomas Becket, dressed richly in his robes, with a few of his priests, is quietly preparing to say Mass. Their movements are careful and silent. The only noise comes from the rustle of their robes.

Suddenly the peace is shattered. There is uproar outside the church, clashing of weapons, the panic of terrified monks. Four men are at the door. They are dressed in full armour. They carry swords, axes and hatchets.

This is how one of the archbishop's attendants describes what happened next:

(1) Finding the doors of the Cathedral barred, they turned aside by a private path through an orchard, till they came to a wooden doorway which they hacked down. Terrified by the uproar, the priests of the Cathedral were scattered like sheep before wolves; but the monks dragged and pushed the unwilling Thomas into the inner church and made haste to fasten the bolts of the folding doors which led into it. . . .

Straightaway these sacrilegious men, with their swords drawn and their armour clashing, entered the church and cried, 'Where is Thomas Becket, traitor to the king and realm?' Whereupon, quite undaunted, Thomas came down the steps near the High Altar and said, 'Here am I, no traitor to the King, but a priest. What do you seek from me?' They demanded that he yield to the King's requests, but he fearlessly refused.

Then they made a rush at him, pulling and dragging him roughly and violently, trying to get him outside the walls of the church and there kill him.

The archbishop, however, clung to a pillar and they could not move him.

Suddenly he recognised one of his assailants and said, 'Touch me not, Reginald; you owe me obedience, but you are acting like a madman.' This Reginald became more angry and violent and said, 'I owe you no obedience which conflicts with my obedience to the King.' Then the unconquered martyr inclined his head as one in prayer and joined his hands together.... He was then struck twice on the head, but still he remained firm on his feet. At the third blow he fell to his knees and with the fourth his head and brains and blood covered the Cathedral floor. Whereupon the knights made off, one of them crying, 'Let us away; this fellow will rise no more.'

In all his suffering, Thomas was incredibly brave. Neither with hand nor robe did he oppose the fatal strokes. Nor when smitten did he utter a single word, neither cry nor groan.

Questions

1 Why does the author say the men wanted to murder Thomas?
2 What is the author's opinion of (a) Thomas (b) the murderers? Which words best show his opinions?
3 List three points which tell you that the author was actually present at the murder. Can you suggest who the author was? Here is a description of what happened to him:

The wicked knight leapt suddenly on the Archbishop and wounded him, and by the same stroke he almost cut off the arm of him who tells the story. For he, when all the others had fled, steadfastly stood by the saint and held his arms around him, till the one arm was almost severed.

4 Is there any suggestion in the account that Becket refused to try to escape? Another eye-witness of the murder added this to his story:

Had he wished, the Archbishop might easily have saved himself by flight. For both time and place offered him opportunity. It was evening. The Crypt was near at hand where there were many dark and winding passages. There was also another door through which he might have climbed to the roof.... But none of these ways of escape would he take.

Who was Thomas Becket?

Thomas Becket was born in London on 21 December 1118. His parents had come originally from Normandy but lived in London. They were fairly wealthy. Many legends surround his birth. One tells how before he was born his mother had a dream that she would give birth to Canterbury Cathedral.

Thomas studied at home, in London schools and at the priory of Merton in Surrey. After he finished his studies in Paris, he became accountant to the Sheriffs of London. He also learned to hunt and hawk. When he joined the household staff of Theobald, Archbishop of Canterbury, he was sent on a number of missions, including two to the pope in Rome.

What was he like as a man? Here are two descriptions of him. The first was written during Thomas's lifetime by an English monk:

(2) Thomas was handsome, tall of stature, with a prominent nose, nimble and active in his movements, clever and very witty and eloquent of speech. He was friendly to all, compassionate to the poor and oppressed, courteous and kind. He wanted all men to respect him; he was ever on guard against deceiving men or being deceived by them.

The second description comes from folk tales, handed down by word of mouth from father to son:

(3) He was now two and twenty years of age, slim of body, pale of skin, with dark hair and a long nose. He was keen of thought, winning in conversation, but slightly stuttering in his talk, and of a wondrously strong memory.

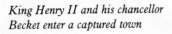

King Henry II and his chancellor Becket enter a captured town

Questions

1 Write out each of the following statements and say whether you think each is fact or opinion.
   (a) Thomas was handsome;
   (b) he was friendly to all;
   (c) he was now two and twenty years of age;
   (d) he was slim of body, pale of skin, with dark hair.

2 Make a list of the points on which the two descriptions agree.
3 What things does Document 2 tell you which Document 3 does not?
4 Which document would you be more likely to believe? Why?

In 1154 the new king, Henry II, made Thomas his chancellor. He became a close companion of the king. They hunted together, sat in court together, decided matters of state together.

Then in 1162 Archbishop Theobald of Canterbury, the head of the church in England, died. There had been many quarrels with the church in the past. King Henry wanted a friend he could trust, as archbishop. He asked Thomas. At first Thomas refused, but under pressure from the king he finally agreed.

(4) Suddenly and dramatically he changed both his dress and his manner. He became very pious. In the following year he went to visit the Pope in France. He told the Pope that he was very worried because he had been given such a high church office from the king, a man who had no right to give it. The Pope soothed his anxiety and said that he, as Head of the Church, confirmed him in his office.

Now dressed in a hair-shirt of the roughest kind, which reached to his knees and swarmed with vermin, he ate very little, chiefly bread, and his normal drink was water used for the cooking of hay.

Why did King Henry and Thomas quarrel?

After visiting the Pope, Becket returned to England:

(5) When Thomas returned to England a quarrel broke out between him and the King. The King had been told by his judges that many robberies and murders had been committed by priests: in fact priests had done more than a hundred murders during Henry's reign. Now these priests had not been properly punished, because they were tried only by a bishop who gave them a light sentence, not by the king's judges who would sentence them to death. As a result of this, churchmen, who ought to give a good example to all, have the chance to commit any crimes they wish.

The King therefore passed new laws against those priests who committed crimes and tried to get the approval of the bishops of the realm. He persuaded them by flattery or terrified them by threats so that all but one agreed. The one who stubbornly refused was Thomas Becket. And because he did so, the King became raging and violent and the Archbishop was forced to flee the very next day to the safety of the court of the King of France.

Thomas spent the years 1165–70 in exile. During that time he found his former friend a most terrifying opponent. One man gave Becket this advice about Henry:

(6) You are dealing with a man whose power and cunning are dreaded, a man

who hates anyone to disobey him, who is easily angered and who will never be told what to do. . . . He is a great king, for he stands in awe of no one and none of his subjects can resist him.

Becket, however, refused to give in. In 1166 he wrote this letter to Henry:

(7) These are the words from the Archbishop of Canterbury to the king of the English. . . .

Since it is certain that all kings, however powerful, receive their power from God, so you as a king do not have the right to give orders to bishops or to drag priests into your royal courts, because bishops and priests also receive their power from God.

Henry also refused to yield. In 1170 he arranged to have his eldest son crowned not by the Archbishop of Canterbury as was usual, but by the Archbishop of York. This was a deliberate insult to Thomas. Later that year, however, Thomas returned to Canterbury during a truce.

Why was Becket murdered? Why did he refuse to flee?

The quarrel finally came to a head when Thomas returned to Canterbury. Here he excommunicated [cut off from the church] all the bishops who had supported Henry during Thomas's exile. The bishops were furious. Many met the king at Poitiers in France:

Inside Canterbury Cathedral where Becket was killed

(8) The King asked the bishops for their advice. . . . At length one of them said, 'My lord, while Thomas lives, you will not have peace or quiet or see good days.' At this the King was overcome with much fury, bitterness and passion against the archbishop. His face and manner became violent. Eager to win his favour, four knights of his household came together and swore to see the Archbishop dead, and left the court.

The four sailed from different ports and met in the castle of Saltwood in England. Before this, however, the Archbishop received news that murderers were soon to arrive. Finding great consolation in the Lord God, he kept the matter secret, lest a tumult should arise at the season of Christmas. On Christmas Day he celebrated High Mass and preached a splendid sermon to the people. He said that the Church of Canterbury already had one Archbishop, St Alphege, who was a martyr, and it was possible that in a short time they would have yet another.

This drawing of the murder was done soon after Beckett's death

On 29 December, the four knights entered the cathedral and murdered the archbishop.

Questions

1 One writer who saw the murder says, 'When the king realised that the four knights had left the court, he issued a warrant for Becket's arrest and gave orders to stop the knights.' What does this tell you that Document (8) does not?

2 What evidence is there, in Documents (1) and (8) (pages 90 and 94), that Thomas actually wanted to die?

3 Who was chiefly to blame for the murder of Thomas Becket: the bishops, the knights, Henry or Thomas himself? Give reasons for your answer.

8 The king's government

The royal household

Medieval government was totally different from that of today. In the Middle Ages a king spent much of his time travelling around his lands on horseback. He had no real capital city and no Parliament to make laws. Only a small number of churchmen, or clerks, could read and write. They ran the government departments of Exchequer and Treasury, and manned the Civil Service. In addition there was no regular army to fight in wars, only a hastily summoned group of knights who owed the king 'military service' (see page 100). It was important, therefore, that a king should be able and strong enough to rule person-

St Louis, King of France (1226–70), gives justice to his people

ally. As he travelled round his realm he was followed by clerks, courtiers and servants. Here is one description of Henry II's travels:

Although his legs are bruised and red from hard riding, he never sits down. . . . On a single day, if necessary, he travels a journey of four or five days. He does not loiter in palaces like other people, but, hurrying through his provinces, he investigates what is being done everywhere, and he is particularly strict in his criticisms of the judges he has appointed in his courts. He always has his sword and dagger with him.

If the king has promised to stay anywhere for the day, you may be sure that he will be up in the middle of the night and set off for somewhere else. Immediately everywhere is confusion: men run about like mad, chariots crash into each other and pack horses are quickly loaded. . . . When we are nearing our destination, the king will stop and decide to stay the night in some other place where perhaps he has only one house and food for himself. We then wander about searching for some filthy pig sty in which we stay the night.

This is very different from the huge buildings of modern London, Washington or Moscow where many important men gather to conduct the affairs of their countries.

The king's duties

If they were strong personalities medieval kings had great power, much more than most presidents or kings have today. They often led their armies into battle. A great soldier like Richard the Lionheart was usually considered a great king, even if he spent hardly any of his reign in England.

Kings also had to give justice to their subjects, to protect innocent people against criminals, murderers and thieves. They had to provide laws and lawcourts so that quarrels and disputes, particularly about the ownership of land, could be settled. The king, in theory, owned all the

St Louis, like Henry II of England, was constantly on horseback. Here he reads prayers while on a journey.

land, but gave much of it away to his important barons. In return the barons assisted him by doing military service whenever he fought a war.

Government departments

The king's government was run by the clerks and knights who made up his household. By the twelfth century they were divided into a number of departments. The Chamber under its chamberlain looked after the king's money and jewels – as it had ever since the days when the king had kept his treasure under his bed for safety at night. The Chancery wrote and dispatched the king's letters. Copies were kept of them as well as of those letters which the king received. It consisted of three or four clerks under a chancellor.

The butler originally chose and tasted the king's wines. Gradually he became responsible for all the provisions needed by the court. Running the household was a major job and large numbers of servants and minor officials all had to be looked after. This account was written in 1136 and describes some of the allowances which had to be paid out:

Twenty servants each one penny a day. Four hornblowers threepence each. Those who help the greyhounds threepence each.... The royal keeper of hounds eightpence a day.... The feeder of the hounds fivepence.... The stoker shall always live in the king's household and throughout the winter he shall have fourpence a day for the fire.

The king and his household had other important jobs too. For example, they were responsible for coining new money and seeing to it that men did not clip the silver from the edges of old coins. This was so widespread that in 1125 'a man who had a pound in the market could only buy twelve pennyworth of goods with it'. Eventually King John had to order his sheriffs in 1205 to collect all the bad money and issue new coins with a ring around the edges to prevent their being clipped.

An Exchequer tally. This was a record of money paid into the Exchequer. The writing recorded the name of the person. The notches tell how much money was paid.

The King's Court

The King's Court (in Latin *Curia Regis*) was always full of barons and bishops who were trying to influence the king. On three occasions each year, at Christmas, Easter and Whitsuntide, the king summoned together all the chief men of the realm to a great feast. He would then wear his crown and royal robes. At these meetings the country's problems were discussed and advice was given to the king on what to do. Some barons might be sent for at other times when the king needed help with a particular problem.

The Exchequer was also a part of the King's Court. One twelfth-century writer described it as:

A large rectangular board, about three metres long and one-and-a-half-metres wide, used as a table by those who sit round it. Over the board is spread a cloth, black but marked with stripes a third of a metre wide. Between the stripes counters are placed. At one end of the table the King's treasurer sits, while to the other the sheriff of each county comes once a year to present his accounts. Along both sides sit the judges, who see that the sheriff has been fair.

The sheriff collected all the taxes in his shire or county. He also collected the fines which criminals paid, and the taxes which the king needed to go on crusades or to ransom himself if he were captured by an enemy.

The Court of the King's Bench. The justices are at the top, clerks and lawyers in the middle, and the accused, in chains, at the bottom.

The law

The sheriff also had to greet the king's two justices when they came to the shire. During the reign of Henry II they visited each shire perhaps once every two years. A meeting of the King's Court was held in a huge hall, with one justice hearing cases at one end of the hall, the other at the other end. There were two types of law cases in the Middle Ages. The first was a criminal case where a man or woman was accused of committing a crime like murder, theft or arson. The second was a civil case where two people were quarrelling, perhaps over the ownership of a piece of land. Henry II developed a system to deal with both.

For criminal cases each county chose twelve important local men to form a 'jury'. After taking an oath they presented to the sheriff any local people who were thought by their neighbours to have committed a serious crime. The accused were brought before the justices, but it was left to God to decide whether they were innocent or guilty. This was done through ordeal. The accused were asked to hold a red-hot iron bar or to put one hand in a cauldron of boiling water. If after several days the burns or blisters had turned septic, they were guilty; if they had not, the accused were innocent. Alternatively, the accused might be thrown into a pond with their hands and feet tied. If they sank they were judged to be innocent, but if the water rejected them and they floated then they were guilty. For the barons there was a further possibility – trial by combat. An accused noble might offer to prove his innocence by fighting for his name, though usually he hired a 'champion' to do it for him! Once guilt or innocence had been decided the justices passed

Trial by combat

An execution

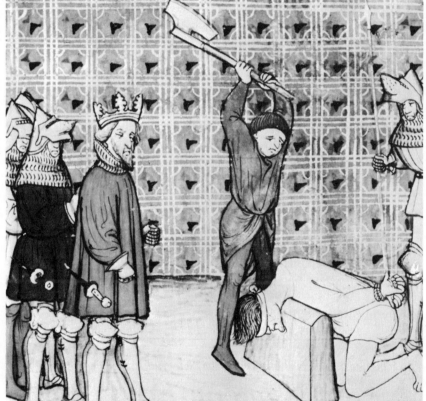

sentence. The usual punishment was a heavy fine, but hanging, banishment and mutilation were also common.

After the event, it was difficult to discover what had actually happened and, if a crime had been committed, who was responsible. How do we investigate today? Trial by ordeal was a very rough and ready way of deciding guilt. Today a man or woman is assumed to be innocent unless they can be proved guilty, but in the Middle Ages there was no proper police force to provide evidence and arrest suspects. However, many people were unhappy with the trial by ordeal and it was banned in the early thirteenth century. Instead juries nearer the kind we have today were introduced.

Juries were also used in civil law cases. Any man who felt he had been wronged – perhaps he thought a neighbour had stolen some of his land – could apply to the King's Court for a 'writ'. This was a letter of command which the king sent to the local sheriff, telling him of the dispute and asking him to bring the case to court. When the case was brought before the justices, twelve local men were again asked to appear, this time to act as witnesses. They would say on oath who, in their opinion, held the right to the land. The justices then gave their verdict accordingly.

Of course there were many other courts operating in England as well as the King's. You can read about the manor courts and the merchant courts in chapters 11 and 12.

The army

English kings had several ways of getting an army together. The only men really skilled in war were the knights and barons, who practised in tournaments and could afford the expensive horses and armour required in battles. Most of the important barons in England owed military service to the king. If their lands were small, then they might be required to serve, with perhaps five or ten fully equipped knights, in the king's army for forty days every year. If their lands were larger, they provided as many as one hundred knights.

In 1166 Henry II drew up a list of the number of knights each baron owed him. This was a great help to the king, but forty days was a very short time. Henry therefore began to allow his barons to pay a sum of money instead of doing the service. With this money the king would hire a troop of mercenary professional fighters, perhaps from Flanders or Brabant on the Continent. These men often plundered local people instead of fighting the king's enemies. The English kings used them mostly in foreign wars.

The Angevins in England

King Henry II of England (1154–89) was the son of Geoffrey, Count of Anjou (hence the name Angevin), and Matilda, the daughter of Henry I. As such he inherited a huge empire consisting of England, Normandy, Anjou, Maine and Touraine. In addition he married

The tomb of Eleanor of Aquitaine at Fontevrault

King Richard the Lionheart

Eleanor, Countess of Aquitaine, and so added that vast territory to his empire. Henry governed his empire well, bringing peace, justice and a number of changes in government. However, he could never really keep his family happy. He and Eleanor had four sons, Henry, Richard, Geoffrey and John, and they could not agree as to which should succeed to the throne when Henry died. The sons, joined by King Philip of France, sometimes rebelled against their father and it was after one such revolt in 1189 that Henry died.

He was succeeded by Richard, known as 'Coeur de lion' or 'Lionheart'. He was a popular warrior king who spent just six months of his ten-year reign in England. The rest was devoted to crusading and wars against King Philip of France. It was during his absence that the outlaw Robin Hood is said to have lived in Sherwood Forest. Robin Hood rallied Englishmen in favour of Richard against Prince John and his supporter the Sheriff of Nottingham.

When Richard died, John became king of England. He was no soldier but a cunning and sometimes violent ruler. His reign (1199–1216) was torn by quarrels. In 1204 he lost Normandy to King Philip of France after a quarrel with some of his barons in Aquitaine. In 1206 he refused to accept the election of Stephen Langton as Archbishop of Canterbury and thus quarrelled with the pope. The climax came, however, in 1215. His English barons were so annoyed by his heavy taxes, military weakness and personal unpopularity that they rebelled. They forced John to accept Magna Carta on the island of Runnymede in the Thames, and he agreed to govern the country fairly and justly. But in case John failed to keep his promise the barons appointed twenty-five men who were to raise an army against him if necessary.

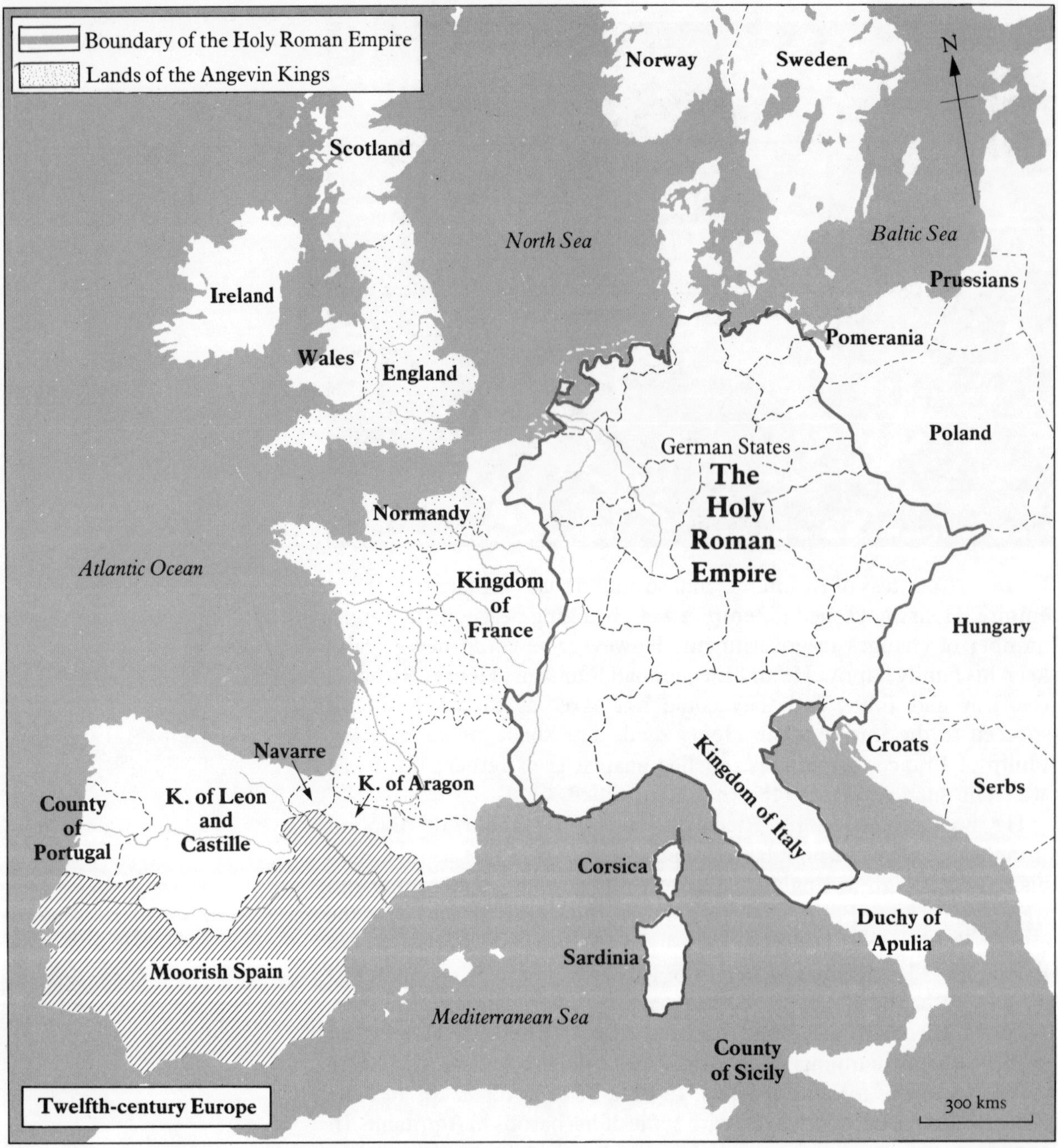
Boundary of the Holy Roman Empire
Lands of the Angevin Kings
Norway
Sweden
N
Scotland
North Sea
Baltic Sea
Ireland
Prussians
Pomerania
Wales
England
Poland
German States
The Holy Roman Empire
Normandy
Atlantic Ocean
Kingdom of France
Hungary
Navarre
Croats
K. of Aragon
Kingdom of Italy
Serbs
County of Portugal
K. of Leon and Castille
Corsica
Duchy of Apulia
Sardinia
Moorish Spain
Mediterranean Sea
County of Sicily
Twelfth-century Europe
300 kms

The countries of Europe

The countries we know today as England, France, Germany, Italy and Spain did not exist as separate states in the Middle Ages. As we have seen, Henry II ruled parts of modern France as well as England. In France the Capetian family had begun their rule in Paris in 987 when the last of Charlemagne's descendants died. But they ruled only a small area around the city and it was nearly three hundred years before the

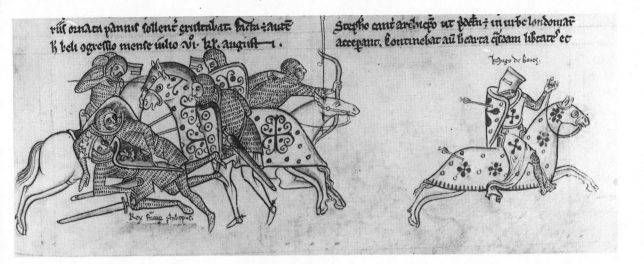

Capetians could conquer, inherit or buy the rest of modern France. Indeed in the fourteenth century, at the time of the Hundred Years War, Gascony still belonged to the king of England, and the port of Calais remained English until 1558.

The battle of Bouvines, 1214. The English leader, Hugh de Bores, flees before the army of King Philip II of France.

The Spanish peninsula was divided into a number of small kingdoms, the largest of which was Castile. It was not until 1492 that the Moslem invaders, described in chapter 3, were finally driven from the south.

In central Europe, the divisions were even more numerous. Instead of the single countries of Germany and Italy, there were a large number of independent princes and city-states who made up the Holy Roman Empire. In the south a group of Normans had built a strong kingdom in Sicily. Central Italy was ruled by the pope from Rome and Lombardy was divided among the wealthy trading cities, chief among which were Milan and Venice. Farther north, the 'muddy towns' and 'gloomy forests' of Germany were ruled by a number of princes called dukes.

The whole area was governed by the Holy Roman Emperor: here is a description of perhaps the most powerful emperor of the twelfth century, Frederick I, called Barbarossa. In 1159 he met ambassadors from the Italian towns at Besançon:

At the meeting Frederick announced that he wanted to protect every man's rights by his laws. The Archbishop of Milan replied that the towns would accept whatever the Emperor decreed, 'for whatever you decide is law to us.'

Yet even an emperor as powerful as Barbarossa might be opposed by the pope, the princes and the towns. Barbarossa was defeated by them in battle in Legnano in 1176.

The Emperor Frederick Barbarossa

Using the evidence: the death of William Rufus

On a warm summer afternoon, 2 August 1100, the king of England, William II, called Rufus, rode out from his hunting lodge in the New

Forest with a few companions. All day he had been a worried man. The previous night he had had a dream. In it he saw a doctor come towards him. The doctor made a cut in his arm and the blood flowed up to Heaven, where it formed a huge black cloud in front of the sun. William awoke in a panic and called his attendants. What could it mean? He stayed in his chamber all morning.

Later William went out to hunt. With him went his younger brother, Henry, his close friend, Walter Tirel, and a few other companions. At the end of the afternoon William's body was found in a lonely glade with an arrow through his heart. 'A few countrymen recovered the body and took it on a cart to the cathedral at Winchester, the blood dripping from it all the way.'

The death of William Rufus

How did Rufus die? Who was responsible? Here are five clues and three opinions.

(1) William Rufus was the second son of William the Conqueror. When the Conqueror died in 1087, he left Normandy to his eldest son Robert, England to William Rufus, and sum of money to his youngest son Henry. Rufus wanted to get Normandy for himself. In 1100 Robert was returning from a crusade with a young bride who could bear him a child. Henry was jealous of both Robert and Rufus as his chances of succeeding either brother seemed to be growing less.

(2) Walter Tirel did not appear at the end of the afternoon. He was next heard of in France.

(3) Later that afternoon Henry left the New Forest, rode to Winchester, seized the Treasury, and three days later was crowned king of England at Westminster Abbey in a hurried ceremony.

(4) Years later Walter Tirel returned to England and he and his family were given rewards in land and money by Henry.

(5) No one at the time accused Henry of murder.

(A) William of Malmesbury, a monk who wrote later in Henry's reign and always tried to get his facts straight, stated:

After dinner he rode into the forest with a very small number of attendants. Among these the King's closest friend was Walter Tirel. This man alone remained with the King, while the others were widely scattered in the chase. The sun was setting, and the King, drawing his bow, let fly an arrow which slightly wounded a stag which passed before him. . . . At this point Walter aimed at another stag, and thus, unknowingly and without the power to prevent it, he pierced the King's breast with a fatal arrow. The King fell to the ground and thus made his death more speedy.

(B) A. L. Poole, in *Domesday Book to Magna Carta*, wrote in 1962:

Some facts seem to suggest a plot. Tirel fled immediately across the seas. His two brothers-in-law, Gilbert and Roger of Clare, were members of the hunting party. Henry was also there. His actions seem to have been premeditated: he rode straight to Winchester.

(C) H. W. C. Davis, in *England under the Normans and Angevins*, wrote in 1905:

The truth was never ascertained. Tirel, it is true, fled the country. But we know that, in later years, when he had nothing to fear from a confession of the truth, he solemnly denied that he was present when the King was slain. . . .

The man who benefited was Henry, but Henry's enemies would not have hesitated to tax him with assassination if there had been the faintest possibility of making out a case.

Questions and further work

1 Which of the clues suggest that Walter Tirel killed the King? Give your reasons for each.
2 Which of the clues suggest that Henry was involved in a murder? Give your reasons.
3 What evidence, in Opinion A, tells you that William of Malmesbury thought it was a genuine accident? What other evidence in William's story suggests that it really was an accident?
4 What are the opinions of Poole and Davis? Do they have any facts to support them?
5 Imagine you were a detective employed in 1100 to find out how King William Rufus died. Make a list of the things you would need to know. Where do you think you would try to find them out?
6 What do you think is the most likely explanation of William Rufus's death? Give as many reasons as you can to support your opinion.

7 Draw a picture of the Exchequer table, using the description on page 98 to help you. Where would the sheriff present his money? How did the sheriff raise the money to put on the table? Why was the table called the Exchequer?
What does the modern Exchequer do?
8 Read this chapter again carefully. Make a list of the various duties and jobs a medieval king had to do. Who performs these duties in England today?

9 The Crusades

The Children's Crusade 1212

In 1212 King Philip of France received a visit from a twelve-year-old shepherd boy called Stephen of Cloyes. He brought with him a letter which he said he had received from Jesus Christ. This letter told Stephen to encourage the children of France to go on a crusade to free Jerusalem from the Moslems. The Mediterranean Sea would dry up and the children would be able to walk unmolested to the Holy Land.

King Philip did not believe in the boy's claims and told him to go home. Pope Innocent III, however, said, 'these children put us all to shame'. In June 1212 about 30 000 children met at Vendôme without food, supplies, maps or arms. Pathetically they marched south to the port of Marseilles. Many deserted or died on the road from lack of provisions. The sea at Marseilles did not dry up as Stephen had promised. Instead, two sea captains, William the Pig and Hugh the Iron, offered to transport the children free of charge to the Holy Land. The fleet did not sail east, however, but south to Africa where all the surviving children were sold to the Moslems as slaves. It is said only one, a young priest, ever returned to France and that was after eighteen years in slavery.

The Children's Crusade

The reasons for the Crusades

Crusades had sailed to the Holy Land long before 1212. Jerusalem, and particularly the Church of the Holy Sepulchre, was a major centre for Christian pilgrims. They believed that it was good for them to journey across Europe to see Bethlehem where Jesus Christ was born, the Mount of Olives and other places where he lived and preached.

The city of Jerusalem according to a later medieval manuscript

The Moslems in the Holy Land

However, it was not easy to reach the holy places. In 632 the Moslem armies, described in chapter 3, conquered this area. All Christians had to pay a poll tax or become Moslems. In addition, many Christian churches were destroyed or rebuilt as mosques. Only Nazareth, Bethlehem and Jerusalem remained largely in Christian hands.

In 1071 a new Moslem ruler appeared in the Holy Land, Malik Shah, the leader of the Seljuk Turks. That year his forces defeated the Byzantine Army at Manzikert and captured Jerusalem. He was much fiercer than previous Moslem rulers and refused to let any Christian pilgrims visit the Holy Land.

Because of this, the Byzantines began to fight back. But they faced one major problem. Many of their soldiers had been killed at Manzikert and the Seljuks had captured Armenia where new recruits were usually found. The Emperor Alexius turned to the west for reinforcements. He sent an embassy to meet Pope Urban II at Piacenza in 1095.

Pope Urban II

Soldiers in the west were very keen to fight in the Holy Land. They had heard many stories of the cruelties which the Seljuks had committed against Christian pilgrims. In addition there was the possibility of winning glory, riches and new lands. This particularly attracted the younger sons of nobles, who stood little chance of inheriting their family lands in England or France.

Christian knights had, in fact, been fighting against the Moslems for some time: the Norman sons of Tancred d'Hauteville had captured south Italy and Sicily from them, and the kings of Castile had reconquered much of Spain. Many knights lived for war. Here was a war of which even the Church approved. Therefore, when Pope Urban II went to France to appeal for support for the crusade, many knights were overjoyed.

He went first to Raymond, the powerful count of Toulouse, who agreed to go to fight the Turks. Then he went to a site outside Raymond's town of Clermont to address the princes and people in a speech which has since become famous. He began by describing the cruelties of the Seljuks, who had 'seized the lands of Christians, conquered them in battle, destroyed Christian churches and devastated Jerusalem, plundering and torturing the people'. Urban then reminded the soldiers in his audience of their glorious military history. He spoke of Charles Martel's great victory over the Moslems at Poitiers in 732, and whetted their appetites by describing the wealth of Palestine, a land just waiting to be conquered. Christian knights, he argued, ought to be fighting to recover this land, instead of warring among themselves at home. Any Christians who would go on a crusade would have their property protected by the church in their absence. As his speech ended a great cry of 'Deus le vult' or 'God wills it' went round the audience and men rushed forward to vow their support. News of the event quickly spread throughout the west and a number of armies were prepared.

The First Crusade

Peter the Hermit

The first of these armies was led by a wandering peasant preacher called Peter the Hermit. He was a small man, dirty and with long matted hair.

Peter the Hermit

He always travelled on a donkey. To many people he seemed like Jesus and it was said that men took hairs from his donkey's tail as holy relics. In 1095, soon after the meeting at Clermont, he set off on a preaching tour of France and also sent some of his disciples to do the same in Germany. Within a year they had gained 15 000 peasant followers. They assembled at Cologne.

The life of the peasant was hard, particularly as much farming land had been ruined by the plundering Vikings and Moslems. The year 1094 had been a year of famine, plague and drought. Most of the peasants who went with Peter were destitute, taking their families and their few possessions with them:

It was a marvellous yet laughable sight: a troop of poor folk in two-wheeled carts, drawn by oxen and containing all their possessions. Every time they reached a walled town, the children would ask again and again if this were Jerusalem.

As they moved down the Rhine and Danube rivers, their numbers increased to 40 000 and food ran short. In Hungary famine set in and some soldiers were sent ahead to get some corn at Seribin. When they tried to plunder the town, they were captured and killed by the natives and their bodies hung on the city walls. Later the main body of the army passed the town and when they saw the bodies, killed 4000 Hungarians in revenge.

They then passed through Constantinople but even here continued their plundering. Even a Christian chronicler condemned them:

They behaved disgracefully, sacking the city and burning palaces, stealing lead from the churches and selling it to the Greeks.

The ancient walls of the city of Constantinople

At last in Asia Minor they met the Turks in battle at Civetot: over 17 000 Christian peasants were slaughtered by the Turks. One Byzantine writer said that the only remains of the Peasants' Crusade was 'a mountain of bones, most conspicuous in height and breadth and depth'.

Princes and knights

Soon after Peter the Hermit's band of peasants came the armies of princes and knights. They were mostly French and many, like Baldwin, the son of Count Eustace of Boulogne, were younger sons. These men sold all that they had and took their families with them, in the hope of winning some lands in the East.

Four main armies travelled separately to Constantinople. From the south came Raymond of Toulouse, who marched through Italy and crossed by sea to Byzantium. From the north of France came Robert of Normandy, the son of William the Conqueror, and Hugh of Vermandois, the son of the king of France. They also went through Italy, but their sea journey was ruined by a storm which wrecked part of the fleet. From Germany came Godfrey of Bouillon, who followed Peter the Hermit's route. Finally the Normans of Sicily, led by the huge yellow-haired warrior Bohemund, sailed over to Constantinople.

A crusading knight. Describe his armour, dress and weapons.

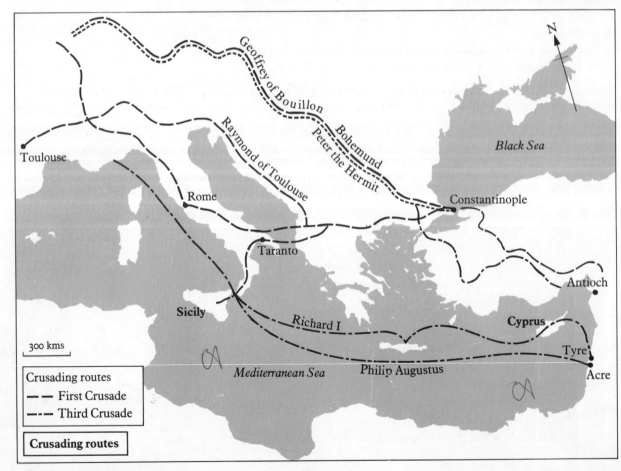

Crusading routes
- – – First Crusade
- –·– Third Crusade

Crusading routes

The armies met at Constantinople. From here they journeyed across Asia Minor towards the Holy Land. The route was hard, as one crusader recorded:

This was a land which was deserted, waterless, uninhabitable. . . . We suffered greatly from thirst and hunger, and found nothing at all to eat except prickly plants which we gathered and rubbed between our hands.

They captured Nicaea, won the battle of Dorylaeum and took Antioch. Then they were besieged by a huge Turkish force in the latter city. The siege lasted for twenty-six days in terrible heat and the crusaders could get no food or water:

Our men ate the flesh of horses and donkeys. So terrible was the thirst that men boiled and ate fig leaves, thistles and even trees.

The army was desperate. As a last resort they sent a weakened force out to face the Turks and after a vital battle they were victorious. Bohemund was made prince of Antioch. The rest of the army marched on to Jerusalem, which was taken with much slaughter in 1099, as the *Gesta Francorum* relates:

So our men entered the city, chasing the Saracens and killing them up to Solomon's Temple where they took refuge and fought hard against our men for the whole day, so that by nightfall all the Temple was streaming with their blood. Many Moslems took refuge on the roof of the Temple, and . . . our men rushed round the whole city seizing gold and silver, horses and mules and houses full of all sorts of goods, and they all came rejoicing to worship at the Church of the Holy Sepulchre.
    Next morning they went up on the Temple roof and attacked the Saracens, cutting off their heads with their swords. Many Saracens committed suicide by throwing themselves headlong off the Temple roof.

The Kingdom of Jerusalem

After their victory at Jerusalem the crusaders captured nearly all of the Holy Land. It was divided into four kingdoms or principalities based on Jerusalem, Antioch, Edessa and Tripoli. In 1100 Baldwin became the first 'King of Jerusalem'. The conquerors settled down to protect their own lands and keep the route to Jerusalem free for Christian pilgrims. Italian cities like Venice, Genoa and Pisa opened markets in coastal towns like Jaffa. Oriental silks, spices and other goods were sent back to Europe. Peaceful trade even grew up with the Moslems. Defence was maintained by a number of well-sited castles.
    For sixty years after the capture of Jerusalem Christians and Moslems lived in peace. This gave the crusaders time to adapt to the desert way of life. Their heavily armed cavalry had found it very uncomfortable and difficult to fight the Moslems in the hot desert. Imagine trying to move quickly in full armour under a burning sun.

The soldier monks

After Jerusalem had been captured, most of the crusading knights returned home to Europe, and there was a shortage of new recruits to

The castle of Krak des Chevaliers. Make a list of the features that made this castle impregnable.

defend the castles of the Holy Land. Fortunately, two large orders of monks were founded early in the twelfth century and by the time of the Second Crusade they could put over 600 fully armed knights into the field. These were the knights of the Hospital of St John, called the Hospitallers, and the knights of the Temple of Solomon, called the Templars. These men took an oath to live like ordinary monks in poverty, chastity and obedience to their Grand Master. They also promised, however, to fight to the death to protect pilgrims and keep the Holy Land free for Christians. St Bernard described the Templars as:

God's servants from among the bravest in Israel, to guard watchfully and faithfully his sepulchre and the Temple of Solomon, sword in hand, ready for battle.

The Orders fought skirmishes against the Moslems, protected convoys of pilgrims, defended castles and showed a great example of courage to the other crusaders. In 1187, for example, at Cresson, a band of three hundred knights rode bravely against the might of Saladin's invading army of seven thousand. One story tells how even the blackest head of hair turned white with terror as the knights were riddled with Moslem arrows and hacked down by swords. Only three of the monks survived.

Saladin

Gradually the Moslems grew stronger. They captured Edessa and in 1146 routed the armies of the second crusade at Damascus. Then in 1171 Saladin became sultan of Egypt. The Moslems had a new, intelli-

gent yet courageous leader and in 1187 his army of 100 000 men completely routed 30 000 crusaders in the desert at Hattin. The way to Jerusalem and the main coastal cities was open and by the end of the year only Tyre and Acre remained in Christian hands.

Saladin was a brave warrior, kind to the poor and generous to his generals. But the Europeans were shocked at the loss of Jerusalem. A new crusade was needed. Its leaders were Europe's three most powerful kings: the Emperor Frederick Barbarossa, a red-bearded giant who had ruled Germany for forty years; Philip Augustus, the cunning and intelligent king of France, and Richard the Lionheart, England's brave

A medieval drawing of Saladin at the battle of Hattin

A desert scene in the Holy Land. It was in this country that Crusaders had to live and fight. What particular difficulties would the land present to them?

A drawing of Richard the Lionheart jousting with Saladin. Stories of such an event were popular in Europe. But, in fact, it never happened.

warrior-king. In 1190 Frederick's army followed the crusader route through Hungary to Constantinople, but their leader was drowned while bathing in Asia Minor and many of his army were killed by plague. Only a few continued to Acre carrying Frederick's body, pickled in vinegar, before them. Philip and Richard travelled together by sea, but quarrelled incessantly before their arrival at Acre. However, their combined army defeated Saladin's and captured the city. Philip, a sick man, then returned home to France.

This left Richard in complete control. Within two years he had captured a long strip of coastal land which he called the kingdom of Acre. In 1192 he and Saladin made peace. Richard was to return to Europe but the Christians kept the kingdom of Acre and pilgrims were to be allowed access to Jerusalem.

The later crusades

Richard's was the last serious attempt to capture Jerusalem from the Moslems, but there were several later crusades. In 1204 the knights of the Fourth Crusade failed to get beyond Constantinople and, after quarrels with the Byzantines, they ransacked the city for three days. This account was written by an eye-witness:

And certain people – who they were I know not – out of malice set fire to the city; and the fire waxed so great and horrible that no man could put it out or abate it. And when the leaders of the army, who were quartered in the other side of the city, saw it they were filled with pity – seeing great churches and palaces falling in, and the great streets filled with merchandise burning in the flames; but they could do nothing.

The tragic Children's Crusade in 1212 was followed in 1229 by the purchase of Jerusalem by Frederick II. The city was held for fifteen years. In 1244 it was lost for good. The only other crusading attempt was made by St Louis of France but he died of fever in 1270 in North Africa. The last Christian stronghold, Richard's kingdom of Acre, was finally lost to the Moslems in 1291.

The death of St Louis

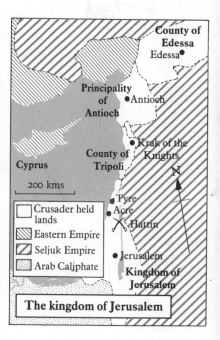

Crusader held lands
Eastern Empire
Seljuk Empire
Arab Caliphate

The kingdom of Jerusalem

The effects of the Crusades on Europe

The early crusades gave many Christians a sense of adventure and excitement when life was hard and usually dull. Stories of bravery and daring were told by returning knights, stories like Richard's victory at Arsuf in 1192. In addition the Italian towns increased their trade with the East, and many princes and nobles gained estates.

Yet the kingdom of Jerusalem and the other principalities were short-lived, and many cruel acts were committed in the name of religion. The later crusades lost sight of the original idea of a crusade and were little more than raiding expeditions. Unscrupulous men exploited the crusaders, many of whom lost their lives fighting in a hostile land. As time went on the crusades became more and more unpopular in Europe.

However, in the long-term, western Europe learnt much from the Moslems: in mathematics, medicine and geography, as well as in the building of castles (and even the military use of carrier pigeons). The design of the castles which Edward I built in the Welsh Marches owed a great deal to the castles built by the crusaders in the Holy Land.

Richard the Lionheart was captured in Austria and forced to pay homage to the Duke. A large sum had to be paid as ransom before he was released and allowed to return to England.

How do we know?

We have very detailed knowledge of the Crusades because many monks retold stories about them. Many of the writers were eye-witnesses and wrote soon after the events they described. This was unusual in the Middle Ages. Much of the evidence, however, is prejudiced, for the Christian or Moslem cause. Joinville's account of St Louis, the monk Ambrose's poem on Richard, or Beha Ed-Din's history of Saladin were all written by men who admired the people they described.

The sites of battles and castles in the Holy Land and surviving siege engines and weapons can still tell us much of the military side.

1071	Seljuk Turks captured Jerusalem
1096	The Peasants' Crusade
1099	First Crusade captured Jerusalem
1187	Battle of Hattin
1190	Third Crusade led by Richard the Lionheart and Philip Augustus of France
1204	Fourth Crusade plundered Constantinople
1212	The Children's Crusade
1291	Crusaders lost the kingdom of Acre

Using the evidence: the siege of Acre (1190)

Victories in the Holy Land were rarely won in open battles. It was more common for the crusading armies to besiege and then capture, a castle or walled town.

In 1190, on the Third Crusade, Richard the Lionheart and Philip Augustus of France besieged the city of Acre. An English monk, Ambrose, described the mining operations used by the crusaders:

(1) The miners were French and they dug so far under the ground that they found the foundations of the walls of the city. They removed a part of these and replaced them with props, to which they then set fire, so that a great section of the wall fell.

Any crusading army, of course, had to get provisions:

(2) First they built with a will
The very first windmill
That was in Syria made.
At sight of it, the race that curses God
Gazed at it agog
And were greatly afraid.

During the siege Richard was taken ill. The monk Ambrose continues:

(3) Although King Richard was not yet fully recovered from his sickness, he was eager for action and determined to take the city. He therefore ordered a huge hurdle to be made, by the most complex workmanship, which was to be used for crossing the trench outside the city.

Under this hurdle he placed his most skilful arbalesters and he himself was carried to the ditch on a silken bed, to honour the Saracens with his presence and put heart into his own men; from his bed he shot many of the enemy by his own skill with the arbalest. In addition his sappers carried a mine under the tower, filled it with logs of wood and set them on fire. A trebuchet also hurled frequent blows at the tower, a part of which suddenly collapsed with a great crash. . . .

Then King Richard ordered the heralds to proclaim a reward of four gold pieces for each stone removed from the City wall. Our soldiers pressed forward immediately, eager for both glory and their reward; but the Turks from the parapets above vigorously repelled them and they had neither shields nor arms to protect themselves. . . .

At last the tower was completely destroyed by the constant attacks of our soldiers, and then our knights, under the leadership of the Bishop of Salisbury, took over: they rode into the city and the Turks ran in dense numbers to press them back. They clashed in hand-to-hand fighting, sword flashed against sword. Our men were but few in numbers while the multitude of the Turks increased constantly, and by throwing Greek fire they forced our men to retreat; some were killed by the enemy and afterwards burned to ashes by the fire. . . .

There still remained in the city 6000 Turks under their leaders Meshtub and Kara-kush, but they were now in need of reinforcements. They therefore sent messengers to our camp, saying that if Saladin did not send them assistance they would surrender the city on the condition that all the Turks should be allowed to depart in freedom. The King of France agreed to this condition, but King Richard absolutely refused and said that after such a laborious siege they should not allow the Turks to leave. . . .

When Saladin heard of this he promised immediate aid, but, because his army did not arrive from Egypt, he was persuaded by his advisers to allow the surrender of the town. As a result the chief men of the city came into our camp and, through interpreters, offered to surrender the city, the True Cross and two hundred and fifty noble Christian captives and five hundred of lesser rank whom Saladin would bring from various parts of the land. As security they offered that all the chief men of the city could be held as hostages.

Philip and Richard had quarrelled yet again. They disagreed further over who was to be the new king of Jerusalem. Richard supported Guy of Lusignan while Philip supported Conrad of Montferrat. After just a few weeks Philip decided to return to France; but the chroniclers disagreed as to why. The French chronicler Rigord said that Philip:

(4) Was then sick of a very grievous illness; besides he looked with suspicion upon the King of England who was sending envoys to Saladin and giving and receiving gifts. . . . Thus after taking familiar counsel with his chiefs, he set his army in order and entrusting himself with sobs and tears to the sea he was carried to Apulia in three galleys given to him by Rufus of Genoa.

The English monk Ambrose, however, painted a different picture:

(5) O how wicked to wish to go away while as yet so much work remained to be done, when his presence was so necessary to encourage the Christians in their holy work. The King of France alleged sickness as the reasons for his return and said that he had performed his vow as far as he was able. . . . Moreover he begged King Richard to supply him with two galleys and the king readily gave him two of his best. It was soon seen how ungrateful he was for his service.

Questions and further work

1 Make a wall time-chart of the Crusades, marking on it the important events, battles, sieges and so on.
2 What problems did the crusaders face in the Holy Land, (see page 111)? What advantages do you think they had?
3 Imagine you were a French knight at the Siege of Acre. Describe the capture of the city in a letter home to your family, referring to the part played by the English and the weapons and methods used in the siege, using the Documents to help you.
4 What did the monk Ambrose think of King Richard? Why do you think his evidence may not be very trustworthy?
5 On what points do the French chronicler, Rigord, in Document 4 and Ambrose in Document 5 disagree about the quarrel between Philip and Richard? Can you suggest why they disagree?
6 What were the main features of the defence of twelfth-century castles? In what ways did the besiegers try to break down these defences?
7 Imagine you are one of the children who joined Stephen of Cloyes in the Children's Crusade. Tell the story of what happened to you up to the moment you found yourself betrayed into Arab hands. How did you feel?

Caerphilly Castle in South Wales. Look closely at this picture and the one of Krak on page 112. In what ways are they similar?

10   The power of the towns

The difficulties of travel

Travel and transport in the Middle Ages were always difficult. There were no concrete roads, of course, and no proper new roads had been built since the time of the Romans. When potholes on existing roads became too deep they might be roughly filled in, but the deep ruts and dust made travel difficult even in summer. In the winter the roads became a sea of mud, making wagon travel almost impossible. Even for the man on foot or horseback there were few bridges or fords across rivers and few opportunities for riders to change horses. Local princes were usually suspicious of travellers. Even a good horseman would therefore be lucky to average fifty to sixty kilometres a day. As late as 1482 Edward IV arranged special relays of riders to take news from Newcastle to London but it still took two whole days. A convoy of packhorses and mules would cover only twenty-four kilometres in a day.

Most long journeys were made by water but here, too, things were awkward. Travellers on most rivers had to pay tolls – there were collecting stations every nine or eleven kilometres on the river Seine, and nearly seventy on the Rhine. Travellers also had to go where the river went.

On the other hand, sea transport was much improved during the Middle Ages. There were new ships, like the sturdy Baltic cog and the hulk, the swift Mediterranean caravel and the carrack. The development of the compass and more detailed maps and charts also helped sailors to find their way. Now a captain did not have to sail from one headland to another; he could go out of sight of land with

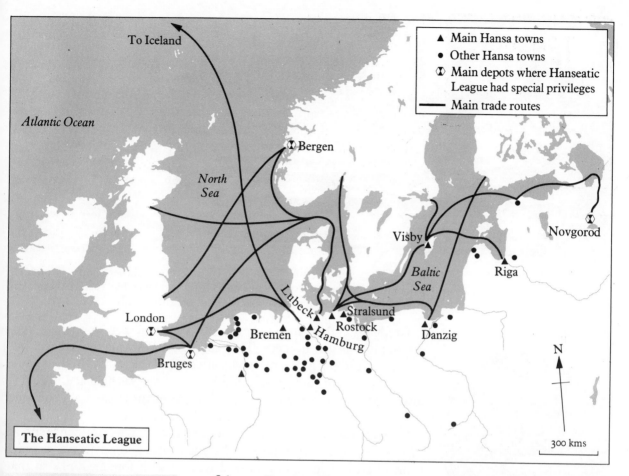

The Hanseatic League

Legend:
▲ Main Hansa towns
● Other Hansa towns
⊗ Main depots where Hanseatic League had special privileges
— Main trade routes

To Iceland

Atlantic Ocean

North Sea

Bergen

Baltic Sea

Visby

Novgorod

Riga

London

Bremen

Lubeck
Hamburg
Rostock
Stralsund

Danzig

Bruges

N

300 kms

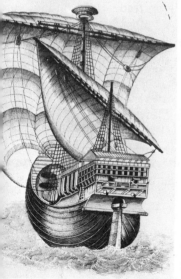

A Baltic cog of the late Middle Ages

confidence. By 1509 Venetian galleys could cover the 4230 kilometres from Southampton to Otranto in Italy in just thirty-one days. As a result of these improvements, important trading towns grew up in three major areas of western Europe: the Baltic coast of north Germany, Flanders and northern France, and northern Italy.

The Hansa towns

The Hansa towns were those on the south Baltic shore from Cologne in the west to Danzig and Riga in the east, and other important towns like Lubeck, Wismar and Stralsund. The town of Lubeck was founded about 1150 close to the trade route which linked the Baltic and North Seas. Trade began with Sweden and Russia but German merchants were soon dealing in furs, timber, cloth and occasionally silver. In 1220 Lubeck traders were given certain privileges in Russia. Other towns rapidly grew up to share them. Wismar (1228), Stralsund (1234) and Danzig (1238) were typical of these.

Soon towns began to group together to defend their convoys against robbers. In 1259 Lubeck, Wismar and Rostock made the following agreement:

We . . . have in common agreed . . . that all who rob merchants on water or on

• LVBECA •

The city of Lubeck

The seal of Lubeck

land shall be outlawed and punished by all cities and merchants. No matter where these robbers go with their booty, no city or land shall receive them. Any city which does receive them shall be cut off from trade.

Gradually other towns began to join together and their representatives began to meet. They talked not only about defence, but also about trading problems which affected all the towns. In the middle of the fourteenth century an assembly of towns was held at Lubeck. It discussed war against Flanders, sailing problems in the Baltic Sea and what action they could take against Baltic pirates.

Soon the League had over 160 member towns. Their influence spread all over Europe as they patrolled trade routes and protected convoys from pirates. They also arranged treaties with foreign kings so that Hansa merchants paid lower taxes on their trade. In London, for instance, the Hansa 'steelyard' or dock was a most favoured area. The League even went to war in 1361 against the king of Denmark. They won easily and destroyed Copenhagen in the process.

But the success of the Hansa towns is best seen in their trading influence. By 1310 they controlled 54 per cent of the wool trade of the town of Boston in Lincolnshire. They also traded salt herrings (the most popular fish all over Europe), Polish wheat, iron from Scandinavia, and had a monopoly of the trade in Russian furs. Every year a huge convoy of ships went to Bordeaux in France for salt. At the other end of Europe in 1336 there were over 160 Hansa merchants at Novgorod in Russia.

The towns of Italy

Until the eleventh century the Mediterranean Sea was largely ruled by the Moslem fleets which sailed from North Africa. In 1015 they were still raiding the north coast of Italy. Gradually the Italian towns began to form their own fleets, and ships from Pisa and Genoa were able to destroy a Moslem flotilla off Sardinia in 1016. This was the beginning of a great revival. The Italian cities began to dominate the Mediterranean and influence the trade of most of the known world.

They grew partly as a result of the Crusades (see chapter 9). In 1087, Genoa, Pisa, Salerno and Amalfi took part in a sea crusade which captured part of the coast of Tunisia from the Moslems. When Godfrey of Bouillon and his soldiers captured Jerusalem on the First Crusade in 1099 the towns saw great opportunities for trade. They could help the crusaders by carrying supplies and recruits to the Holy Land and protecting its shores against Moslem naval attack. Pisa sent 120 ships in 1099 and Venice a fleet of two hundred a year later. Perhaps the most important event occurred in 1123 when a huge Venetian convoy of three hundred ships completely destroyed an Egyptian fleet off Ascalon.

In return for their help the towns demanded booty, markets, warehouses and trading rights in nearly all of the captured cities of the East. They thus grew rich as a result of the Crusades. Many of them traded with the Moslems. In 1154 Pisa even sold arms and war materials to the

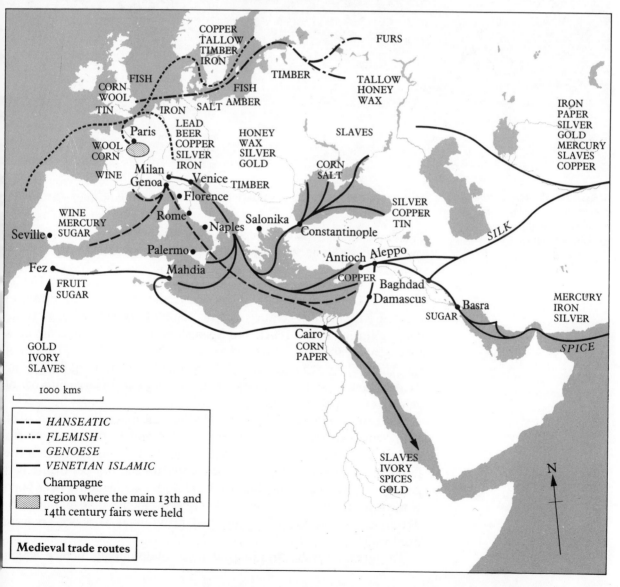

Medieval trade routes

Venice. Describe the different ships. Gondolas, like the one in the foreground, are still used on the lagoons of Venice today.

sultan at Cairo. By the mid-twelfth century one German chronicler could write:

Practically the entire land is divided among cities . . . and scarcely any noble can be found who does not acknowledge the authority of his city.

On the western side of Italy, the two great trading cities were Genoa and Pisa. Genoa was chiefly interested in the western Mediterranean trade. By the twelfth century she was claiming the control of all trade passing through the French and Spanish ports. In the thirteenth century Genoese trade was extended to include North Africa and later even the Atlantic. By 1424 Genoa had the second largest trading fleet in the Mediterranean: sixty-three large transport ships and a large number of galleys to provide protection.

Pisa concentrated on the central Mediterranean, on the corn trade of Sicily and Sardinia, and on bringing wool and leather from North Africa. She was, however, defeated by her rival, Genoa, in 1282 at the important battle of Meloria. By the fourteenth century her wealth had passed to Florence. Here fine woollen cloth was made by over 6000 workmen. In Florence, too, many improvements in banking were developed by the Medici family, and many great works of art were produced.

The greatest Italian trading city was undoubtedly Venice which began to control the profitable spice trade from the East. In 1204 the Fourth Crusade set off from Venice, but instead of sailing against the Moslems it attacked and plundered Constantinople. As a result Venetian merchants controlled the wealth and trade of that city for a further fifty years. Venice made treaties with cities all over the East (like Trebizond and Tara on the Black Sea and Alexandria in Egypt) and Venetian merchants like Nicolo Polo and his son Marco, went even farther afield.

Twice a year the 'Flanders galleys' now set sail from Venice, carrying the wealth of the East, spices, pepper, sugar, to the north of Europe by way of Gibraltar and Southampton to Bruges. They returned to Venice with timber, furs, English and Flemish wool, and wines. The Venetians were the greatest traders in Europe.

The northern fairs

The industry and trade of north-western Europe in the Middle Ages was based on wool. The best wool was produced in England, on the huge estates of the Cotswolds in the west and the vast Cistercian lands in Yorkshire in the north. By the twelfth century, English wool was being exported, mostly to Flanders, to the major towns of Ypres, Ghent and Bruges. There it was manufactured into fine quality cloth and finished ready for the markets of Europe and the Mediterranean.

Woollen cloth was a high quality product, not too bulky for the poor state of medieval transport, but very profitable for the manufacturer.

An Italian merchant and a banker. Describe what you think the people in these pictures are doing.

The towns of Flanders. What does the picture suggest were the main features of Flemish towns and trade?

English merchants and kings soon realised how valuable their wool was. They decided to fix a number of 'staple' towns as centres for the sale and distribution of wool to Flanders. Merchants could thus concentrate on one town and kings could more easily tax the export of wool. The staple was placed at various times at Antwerp, Bruges, Boston and other towns, and finally centred on Calais. In 1354 the 'Merchants of the Staple' were incorporated into a company, which organised convoys and agents in foreign cities to protect and improve trade.

The Flemish cities of Bruges, Ghent and Ypres became large industrial areas with much power. During 1313 Ypres alone produced over 92 500 cloths and a large variety of cloth types was made. Bruges concentrated on light fine cloth while Ghent was famous for the heavier scarlet material. The Old Hall of Bruges was over eighty-three metres high and demonstrated the power of the Flemish towns. After being made and finished, Flemish cloth was taken to the fairs of Champagne, held in four towns in northern France: Lagny, Bar, Provins, and Troyes.

To these great markets came merchants from all the Italian cities. They brought spices and the goods of the East, alum (obtained from Egypt and necessary in the making of cloth) and various dyes, like woad

The belfry at Bruges

The wool trade

and brazil-wood. These were exchanged for cloth which was then taken to Italy. From there it was distributed throughout the Mediterranean. Hansa merchants also came to Champagne. Whole villages were built with special stone cloth-halls to accommodate the many travellers. Even the roads through France led to Champagne, and Alpine passes, like the Great St Bernard, were crossed throughout the year by merchants travelling there.

How do we know?

We know very little about the great towns of the Middle Ages. We can only guess at their population, their size, their trade and their power, although the work of archaeologists into the size of town walls, and the records of customs duties and other taxes levied by governments do tell us something. It is not until the fourteenth century, however, when laymen began to write, that we really begin to see how trade was conducted between the great towns.

Using the evidence: English overseas trade

In the later Middle Ages, English kings were particularly anxious to protect the trading rights of English merchants. This Navigation Act was passed in 1382 by Richard II:

(1) Also, to increase the navy of England, which has recently become much smaller, it is agreed that none of the subjects of our lord the king shall henceforth ship any kind of merchandise into or out of the realm but only in ships of the king's allegiance.

The same king in 1398 sent the following letter to all naval officials in England:

(2) Know that . . . our beloved Antonio Bragadino and Andrea Sisi, the masters of two Venetian galleys now in the port of London, may enter our kingdom with their goods and merchandise, and also other masters from Venice. Provided they pay our customs and excise on merchandise which they expose for sale and provided they pay promptly for victuals which they trade.

The merchants of the Hanseatic League were particularly favoured in England. The following agreement was made with them in 1437:

(3) All German merchants of the Hanse ought to use and enjoy all the privileges and freedoms granted to their predecessors by kings of England . . . and no new exactions or subsidies shall be imposed on their persons or goods.

Wool was the commodity most commonly shipped abroad, always in the fifteenth century to Calais, the staple town. This letter of 1481 reveals how it was done:

(4) Right worshipful sir, I humbly recommend myself to you. My master has shipped his fells which you must receive and pay the freight. First, by the grace of God, in the *Mary* of London, William Sordyvale master, 7 packs, lying by aft

A crane used at Bruges.
How did it work?

Loading the wool fells

the mast, one pack lyeth up rest and some of that pack is summer fells marked with an o. Item, in the *Christopher* of Rainham, Harry Wylkyns master, 7 packs and a half, Cotswold fell, lying be aft the mast. Item, in the *Thomas* of Maidstone, Harry Lawson master, 6 packs, whereof lyeth 5 packs next before the mast under hatches, and one pack lyeth in the stern sheet. . . . Item, sir, ye shall also receive in the *Mary*, Rainham, John Danyell master, your trunk with your glass and an Essex cheese.

Such ships often sailed to Calais in convoy, with some protection. The following account was paid to one William Fethirston who arranged a convoy in 1475:

(5) First, paid the 18th day of March, the aforesaid year, for the convoy of wool and woolfells from the port of London, to William Fethirston, master of the *Carrack* called the King's ship, for the wages of 200 men, every man taking 6s. 8d.—total £66 13s. 4d.

Also, paid for victualling the same men, every man for the space of two weeks at 12½d. a week—total £20. 16s. 8d.

Also, paid to William Fethirston for a ship called the *Burnet* with 50 men—total £22. 1s. 10d.

At the same time wool prices at Calais were fixed.

(6)

March wool	*20 marks*
Cotswold fine	*18 marks*
Lindsey, Berkshire	*16 marks*
Wiltshire, Nottinghamshire	*15 marks*
Warwickshire	*14 marks*
Cambridgeshire, Derbyshire, Hampshire	*13 marks*
Essex, Sussex, Kent	*12 marks*

In 1463 Parliament tried to make sure that all wool for export was of good quality:

(7) Because daily great deceit is done by the owners of wool who put into the fleeces locks of much worse wool than the top fleece is and also put inside the fleece, tar, stone, sand, dirt, to the great damage of the buyer and to the great reproof of the merchants of his realm, the king has ordained that all wool should be properly wound, upon paid of a forfeit, for any default, of sixpence.

The government also faced problems from smugglers. The following charge was made in an inquiry at the Exchequer court:

(8) That Nicholas Styward, Clerk, Vicar of the Church of Rushmere in Suffolk, in a certain creek, placed and hid in a certain ship of Holland 40 quarters of wheat, price of each quarter 13s. 4d. and six barrels of wool grown in the country, each barrel containing six stones of wool, the price of each stone 2s. 6d., and he caused the same merchandise, on the feast of Martinmass, to be carried away to foreign parts, without paying the customs due to the lord king.

In spite of the profits of the wool trade, there were also criticisms of it. The following one was expressed by a Yorkshireman:

(9) Wool and woolfells have passage out of the realm, wherefore all foreigners take but little reward to buy our English cloth, but make it themselves. The remedy is this: let it be ordained that no wool or fell pass out of the country.

Dyeing the wool

Long Melford Church in Suffolk. A number of churches like this were built in the later Middle Ages with money made in the woollen trade.

Questions and further work

1 What kinds of goods were traded in the Middle Ages? Make a list and beside each item explain briefly:
(a) where they came from;
(b) one possible use for them.
For example:

item	from	use
timber	N. Europe	shipbuilding

2 The above nine documents are taken from the following sources. Write out the list of sources and say which documents belong to each source:
(a) An Act of Parliament
(b) a letter
(c) records of the Exchequer Court
(d) a bill of account
(e) a trade treaty
(f) an official price list.

3 Take each of the sources in turn and give reasons why the information was written down – that is, for what purpose was the source written? Which source do you think would be the least reliable for the historian to use here?

4 (a) Which document is a simple statement of facts?
(b) Which document is a simple statement of opinion and contains no facts?
(c) From Document 7 note down one statement of fact and one opinion.

5 Make a list of the difficulties and problems which the government faced in organising the wool trade. How did it try to solve them?

6 Imagine you were a sailor in the *Thomas* of Maidstone. From the information given in this chapter – look closely at the pictures – describe your voyage to Calais, from the loading-up in Maidstone to the unloading in Calais.

Medieval
life

11 Life on the manor

Lord and peasant

The peasant

And when they had finished their work, the lord ordered that they should have meat and drink in abundance. A great tub was set in the Hall and filled with wine . . . and each was to drink for himself. The cellarman locked up his cellar and the cook his kitchen; and if so be that the peasants waxed drunken and attacked the cook, they paid no fine for this deed. They could drink so that two of them could not carry the third back to the wagon.

In the thirteenth century the population of England was about four million, and nine out of ten of these people lived in the countryside. For most of them life was hard. Long hours working in the fields, a very simple diet and cramped and uncomfortable housing were the lot of most peasants. Holiday celebrations like the one described above provided an all-too-rare change from normal everyday life.

The life of the lord of the manor was very different. Everyone who lived in the village owed something to the lord. The free men still had to pay him taxes and life was harder for those who were not free like the villeins. A villein had strips of land in the open fields and perhaps a garden, but several days a week he had to work on the lord's land for nothing. Even so, if the lord was a fair man, the villein might live reasonably and we know that some villeins were better off than the poorer free men of the village.

An overseer watches as peasants bring their corn to be ground at the lord's mill

The villein's cottage

One writer described the villein's cottage as 'a decrepit hovel, with rotten beams and half-ruined walls'. This was often true. The walls were usually made of layers of mud and the roof roughly thatched. The wealthier peasant's house would be larger and better built, using more timber.

Most cottages had one or two rooms. They had holes in the wall instead of windows, and these were covered with wooden shutters in wet or cold weather. This made the cottages very dark inside. There was no chimney as such, only a hole in the roof, and the fire made the room smoky and sooty. It was difficult for people to keep clean, particularly as chickens, cats, dogs and even pigs shared the family home.

Inside, the cottage was very bare. The earthen floor was trodden down hard, but likely to get wet in the winter. Imagine a fire built on an iron plate, in the middle of the room, with a cluster of cooking utensils around it: earthenware pots and pans, metal forks, and wooden basins. Nearby would stand a few wooden stools, a small table and a wooden chest for clothes. The beds were bags of straw covered by a rough blanket, and instead of a pillow, people used 'a good round log under their heads'. Compare this with the so-called luxuries and necessities in our homes today.

Outside the cottage, a villein might have a small garden. Here he

A cruck cottage in Didbrook, Gloucestershire

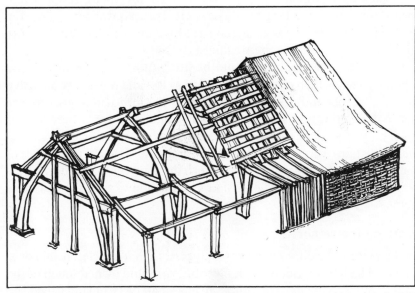

might have apple trees and pear trees and grow a few vegetables: cabbages, leeks, onions, peas and beans. He relied on the garden and his strips in the fields, to feed his family and himself.

The manor house

The lord of the manor usually lived in a much larger house, though by modern standards it also was very poor. It was often built of wood on

The hall inside Stokesay Castle in Shropshire

stone foundations, although later some very grand stone houses were constructed. The main room or hall was a long square room where meals were eaten on a long trestle table. It also served as a bedroom for the lord's servants, and as a playroom for his children. The manor court took place there, too, if the weather was bad.

Quite often the furniture would be little different from that of the villeins'. The earthen floor would get just as wet and the fire would leave deposits of soot and grime everywhere. If the lord had a large manor house it would have a separate bedroom called a bower, where he and his family slept. The lord would have a large four-poster bed, around which curtains were drawn to keep out draughts. Even in the houses of the rich glass windows were rare before the fourteenth century. Shutters and screens were used over doors and windows as in the peasant's home.

Work on the manor

In the picture the different parts of a typical manor are clearly laid out. The lord had his house, garden, mill and barns and owned much of the land in the three fields. The church held a small piece of land called the glebe, and a tithe barn. Here the priest stored the corn which the villagers gave as their tax to the church. The villeins themselves had their huts, gardens, and scattered strips in each field. They also had rights on the common land and if they were particularly energetic they might clear some woodland and wasteland to use for farming. The roads were no more than cart tracks, full of potholes, dusty in summer and muddy in winter.

Farming

The three fields were divided into strips, each about ten metres wide and running where possible the whole length of the field. There would be a small ridge or ditch to separate one strip from the next, but there were constant disputes at the manor court about the stealing of land. Each strip was ploughed with a very heavy wooden plough, pulled by four, six or even eight oxen in heavy soils. The strips were long and narrow to save the oxen from having to turn around too often. Few villeins owned six oxen themselves, so they worked together, each lending one or two animals and helping to plough the strips belonging to his neighbours.

In a manor with three fields, the villeins in a given year would sow barley in one, wheat in another and leave the third fallow or empty so that the soil could recover its goodness. In the following year they would change around, and again in the third year. Every three years each field had one crop of wheat, one of barley and one year fallow. Life was never easy:

The ploughman says: 'I work hard: I go out at daybreak, driving the oxen to the field and I yoke them to the plough. Be it never such a hard winter I dare not linger at home for fear of my lord. Every day I must plough a full acre or more.

My son drives the oxen with a goad iron and he is hoarse with the cold and shouting. And I do more also. . . . I have to fill the oxen's bins with hay and water then and clear them out. Mighty hard work it is, for I am not a free man.'

The villein's working year was a hard one. In January he would spread on the fields what manure he had gained from his animals during the winter. In the spring he would plough and sow the seeds. The fallow field had to be ploughed to keep down weeds. In June hay was cut from the meadows to store as a winter fodder for cattle. Weeding, draining and ditching were constant jobs before the late summer, the joyous time of harvest. It was at this time that a villein and his family had to spend at least three days a week working on his lord's harvest before he could begin his own. This often made villeins angry, but they were given free meals during the time. When the fields were bare, only stubble remained and cattle were put to eat their fill before the land was ploughed over yet again. As winter approached the villein had to calculate how many animals he could feed during the winter. The rest were slaughtered and salted down for meat.

A villein's animals were valuable possessions. The cow was the most valuable: she produced milk, butter and cheese, some of which might be sold, although the yield was poor in wintertime when fodder was scarce. The ox was the best working animal, although the horse was becoming more popular. One medieval writer preferred oxen:

When the horse is old and worn out, then there is nothing but the skin; but when the ox is old, with ten pennyworth of grass he shall be fit for the larder.

If the ox or cow were killed for the winter, both the meat and the hide were used. The pig was a very useful animal, too, which could be fed easily on waste or in the woodlands. Salted bacon or pork was often to be found in a villein's cottage. Finally sheep provided valuable wool, skins, and carcases. In some areas like the West Riding of Yorkshire the villein's wife and family would spin and weave the yarn into cloth themselves.

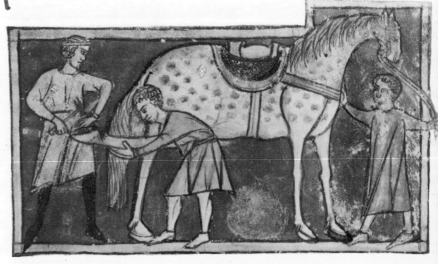

The villein's duties

The heaviest burden on the villein was his duty to his lord. He could not let his daughter marry, sell his animals or grind corn without the lord's permission. If he were caught poaching the lord's fish or stealing a rabbit during the hungry months of February and March he was brought before the manor court where the lord could have him fined. His work in the fields was often watched by the lord's overseer. A manor official, called the reeve, although he was a villein himself, was usually appointed by the lord to see that each villein did his duties properly. Here is a twelfth-century account of the duties of one villein:

From autumn to the beginning of August he works for two days each week on the lord's land and ploughs for a third. And if there is such a hard frost in

Describe this farmworker's dress

winter that he cannot plough, then he works on Fridays instead of ploughing. From the beginning of August until Christmas he works for three full days each week. In winter he ploughs half an acre for the lord and sows it with his own seed; and also another half acre in August.

He makes payments for his rights on the common; he pays 4 pence at Christmas and one halfpenny for wool.

And in August he performs two days' carrying service for corn, one for timber and he does one day's fencing. And when the lord calls for extra work in August he shall come with his whole family and he shall then be fed by the lord.

You can understand the villein's annoyance at all these services, which were particularly heavy during the harvest month of August!

Daily life

The poverty of the villein can be clearly seen from the food that he and his family ate. In the morning he would have perhaps a hunk of bread and a mug of watery ale, at midday the same again, possibly with a piece of cheese or an onion or two to add flavour. The main meal of the day would come in the early evening, consisting of thick soup or pottage. Occasionally, if an animal had been killed, there might be a piece of bacon or a stringy, tough leg from an ox. Only on feast days or when the food was provided by the lord did the average villein eat well. The usual drink was ale or cider.

Recreation

On feast days and church festivals, work ceased and the whole village relaxed. The lord of the manor would go hunting for deer or wild boar or hawking for birds, but the villein's pleasures were simpler. Each Sunday was a holy day, hence our word holiday, when 'no man do any work, except it be good'. There were about twenty other holy days each year, including Christmas, Easter and Whitsuntide. There was dancing around the maypole on Mayday and a bonfire feast on Midsummer's night.

Perhaps Christmas was the happiest season. The festivities would last ten or fourteen days until about twelfth night and villeins' huts would be decorated with holly and ivy. Often the lord provided a huge feast for the whole village in the manor hall. Each villein was required to bring a mug and plate and would receive a white loaf, two kinds of meat and as much good ale as he or she could drink. A mummer's play might be performed and everyone would join in the singing of carols.

> Now make we merry both more and less
> For now is the time of Christmas. . . .

Perhaps the most popular sport in the country was a form of football played between two neighbouring villages. It was often a dangerous game, played over the whole countryside with a hundred or more in each team:

In this game the young men propel a huge ball by striking and rolling it along the ground with their feet. A game which is more undignified and worthless than any other, rarely ending without some loss, accident or damage to the players. The boundaries had been marked and the game started when one man threw himself into the midst of the fray to try to get the ball. Then one of his own side came up against him and kicked him by mistake, missing the ball.

As a result, many lords banned the sport from their manors.

How do we know?

Archaeology and remains which are still visible help us to imagine the appearance of a typical medieval village. In many places there are

This aerial photograph of Middle Ditchford in Gloucestershire, shows where the medieval houses and streets once were

church buildings from this period. Fields with the balks and ridges can still be clearly seen. There are also aerial photographs of villages (especially those now deserted) showing the layout of the cottages and other buildings.

If we add to these sources the written accounts of some manor courts where villagers were tried for minor offences, and the accounts made by stewards or reeves all over the country, we begin to see the work of the village more clearly. By the fourteenth century people other than priests were beginning to write. In poems like Langland's *Piers Plowman* or Chaucer's *Canterbury Tales* we are given views of the life of a village through the ploughman, the reeve, the parson or a wandering friar who may pass by.

Another very useful source is the private letters written by people like the Paston family of Norfolk. These tell us much of personal relations and also the problems of running a large estate, especially in troubled times:

> And as for getting in the money, I never saw a worse season; for Richard Calle saith he can get but little in substance of that which is owing. . . . And John Paston saith they that may pay best they pay worst.
>
> *Margaret Paston to her husband, January 1462*

Using the evidence: The church and village life

At the centre of every village, next to the manor house, stood the church which, with its priest or curate, had a tremendous influence on the everyday life of the villagers. Many priests were themselves poorly educated and not well qualified to set an example to ordinary people:

(1) At Clunbury the parishioners say that Sir Edward, curate of the parish, doth not serve the parishioners duly as he should; nay, rather, he stirreth quarrels and contentions among the parishioners, and doth other detestable things to the scandal of the church. Item, that the said Sir Edward was called upon to administer extreme unction to Richard Crowe on his deathbed; yet he expressly refused to do this. . . . Item, that the said Sir Edward absented himself from the church on the feast of Corpus Christi, so that the parishioners had no divine service. Item, that William, son of John Phyppes, lately deceased, was buried without Mass and burial service, by default of the said curate. . . . Item, that the vicar is bound to find a deacon to serve in the church, which he doth not. . . .

At another parish, Dymock:

(2) The rector is bound by ancient custom to distribute weekly to the poor two bushels of mixed rye and wheat, which hath now been withdrawn for twenty years and more. . . .

Occasionally the priest would give a sermon though in the Middle Ages it was only bishops who preached regularly. Here is an extract from a typical sermon warning the congregation of the horrors of Hell:

A carving on a church door in Italy

This painting comes from Beauvais in France. What is happening in the picture?

(3) Some shall burn in the great flaming of fire which is ten times hotter than any fire in this world. Some shall draw their limbs asunder and smite their bodies with fiery brands. . . . There shall be flies that bite their flesh. . . . There is no sound but horrible roaring of devils, and weeping and wailing and gnashing of the teeth of damned men, crying 'Woe, woe, woe, how great is this darkness!'

For the peasant who could not read or write, this graphic account was very real. Even more memorable were the pictures found in most churches.

Religion was possibly brought most to life in the miracle and mystery plays performed in towns by members of the craft guilds (see chapter 12).

Questions and further work

1 (a) What are the two main opinions stated in Document 1?
  (b) What four pieces of evidence does the writer use to support his opinions?
  (c) From the evidence, do you think that the opinions are fair? Give reasons for your answer.
2 Make a list of four ways which the church used to teach the people about Christianity. Which of these do you think people would take most notice of? Which would they take least notice of?
3 What are Document 3 and the picture on page 144 warning people of?
  (a) Is the hell which the bishop describes a fact or an opinion?
  (b) People in the Middle Ages considered it a fact. Can you suggest, from the evidence here, any reasons why they did so?
4 On a large piece of drawing paper, make a calendar of a villein's working year. Illustrate each part of the year with a drawing.
5 It is easy to see how we today are better off than medieval villagers. Write a short speech using the evidence in this chapter to argue that, in some ways, the villein was happier than the modern worker.
6 The duties of the villein to his lord are clearly set out in this chapter. What were the duties of the lord to his villeins?

Town buildings

Look carefully at the plan. In 1610 Lincoln was still a typical large medieval town. The city wall and the river served as protection. Notice also the small castle at the bottom of the picture, the large cathedral in the centre, and the many churches around the town. You should also realise how small the town is, even in 1610, and how close it is to the surrounding fields and farms.

In the streets

In a town like Lincoln, the streets were very narrow. They were usually just cart tracks with no stone foundation or pavement. Each householder was supposed to clean the piece of road outside his house. Most people threw their rubbish out into the streets instead and an open sewer often ran down the middle of the street into a nearby river. In 1365 the mayor and citizens of Lincoln received a letter from the king:

It has lately come to the king's ears that, because of the mud and dung and filth thrown in the streets and lanes and other loathsome things lying about, foreign merchants seldom come to the town. . . . He therefore urges the citizens to have the streets and lanes of the city cleaned at once.

Butchers often cut up meat in the streets and dead animals could lie around for days unburied. The smell must have been horrible, especially in summer.

Streets of the town were often named after the traders or craftsmen who had their shops there. In medieval London, for example, there was Fish Street, Ironmonger Row and Cornhill. A craftsman would carry on with his work, chat to passers-by and sell his goods from his shop on the

Speed's map of Lincoln in 1610

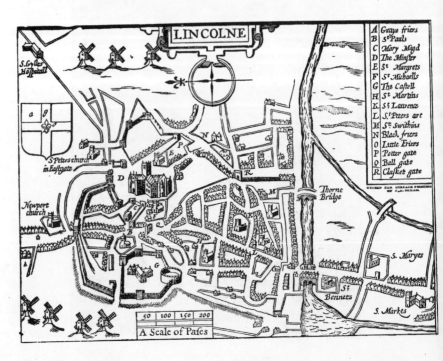

ground floor, while his living quarters and his apprentices' room would be at the back.

Town houses

Houses were built close together on both sides of the narrow streets. It was usual for the upper storey to jut out and overhang the street. In the front of each house was a large hall, often two storeys high, and at the back the solar or private bedrooms upstairs and a storeroom downstairs. The kitchen was often in a separate building to reduce the risk of fire.

Later in the fifteenth century when many merchants became wealthy, they built bigger and better houses. Glass windows replaced wooden shutters and lead roofs and tiled floors came into use, especially in London. The very wealthy had elaborate stone fireplaces and chimneys, French or Italian tapestries on the walls and fashionable ornamental windows.

Most houses had little furniture. There were wooden tables, stools, benches and chests and usually straw beds. Occasionally a wealthy merchant would own a large four-poster bed with a feather mattress and curtains all round to keep out the draughts, and also one or two solid,

Left The Shambles in York. Notice the narrow street, the low open shops and the overhanging upper stories of the houses.

Right In what ways is this medieval street similar to The Shambles?

high-backed wooden chairs for him and his lady when they entertained guests.

Fire was the great danger in a town of wooden buildings and thatched roofs. The city of London was unusual in passing these decrees as early as the twelfth century:

Whosoever wishes to build, let him take care as he loveth himself and his goods, that he roof not with reeds nor rush, but with tile only or with lead. . . . And let old houses in which brewing or baking is done be whitewashed and plastered within and without, that they may be safe against fire. They say also that it is only proper that before every house should be a tub full of water.

Perhaps the best regulation was that any wall dividing two houses should be built of stone. This made it much more difficult for fire to spread.

The origins of towns

The charter given by King Henry III to the City of Oxford in 1229

When the Romans left England in the fifth century most people lived in small villages. But after the Saxon invasions a number of towns grew up. These were usually in important positions near a ford or bridge across a river or on a good harbour. The towns became markets, where the people from local villages could come once a week to buy or sell. In addition, at a time of invasion, men sought shelter and defence behind town walls. King Alfred and his sons built burhs, many of which became county towns – fortified places where money was minted and law courts held.

After the Norman Conquest it was common for townsmen or burgesses to ask the king for a royal charter to make their town a royal borough. Here is part of the charter granted by Henry III in 1229:

Henry, by the grace of God, King of England . . . to all archbishops, bishops, abbots, earls . . . and his faithful people. Take note that we have granted that our town of Leverepul shall be a free borough for ever, and that the townsmen shall have a merchants' guild with liberties and free customs.

The liberties the townsmen gained were many: they were not villeins but free men; they paid no labour services to any lord and had to ask no one's permission to marry, or to grind corn. They were also protected by the borough court which tried any disputes between townsmen. Any villein who escaped from his lord and sheltered in a town for a year and a day was considered a free man. In return for these freedoms, the borough paid the king a sum of money and also a regular tax.

The guilds

Most of the craftsmen and traders living in a medieval town would belong to its merchant guild. Craftsmen wanted to protect their rights against 'foreigners' from other towns. In addition, the merchant guilds laid down rules about the price of goods and honest workmanship. They also defended any member who was imprisoned, and gave food and money to a member who was too ill to work. In 1400 the following

Salisbury traders had their own guilds: grocers and drapers, weavers, fullers, tailors, brewers, shoemakers, bakers, innkeepers, bookbinders, carpenters, bowmakers, builders, barber-surgeons and cooks, goldsmiths and blacksmiths, saddlers, pewterers, butchers and tanners, dyers, painters.

Each guild consisted of a number of master craftsmen, who were fully qualified and experienced workers, and a number of journeymen and apprentices. Craftsmen usually served a seven-year apprenticeship before they became journeymen. They would then continue living in the master's house and work in his shop until they could afford a house and shop of their own. Before they could finally qualify as masters they had to be examined by the guild.

Every guild made strict rules for its craftsmen. For example Lincoln

The Guildhall, Lincoln

Interior of the Guildhall, York

barbers could only charge $\frac{1}{4}$d. for a shave in 1440 or $\frac{1}{2}$d. if the customer was a priest. No member could work on Sundays, feast days or after dark. Any quarrels between members was settled by the guild. In addition any member who fell ill was to receive help:

The Megucers [Mercers] of London have ordained . . . that each person of the said trade shall put in the guild box such sum as he shall think fit. If, by chance, any one of the said trade shall fall into poverty, whether through old age, or because he cannot labour or work, he shall have from the said box 7d. for his support, provided he be of good repute. And after his death, if he have a wife of good repute, she shall have weekly from the said box 7d. for her support, so long as she shall behave herself well and keep single. . . . And if anyone of the said trade shall depart this life and have not wherewithal to be buried, he shall be buried at the expense of the common box.

Guilds of mercers existed in a number of towns. They were dealers in expensive cloths like silk.

Trade

Markets

The important event each week for the craft and merchant guilds was the town market. In the thirteenth century there were over three

A tailor's shop. Notice the dress and the tools. What are the people doing?

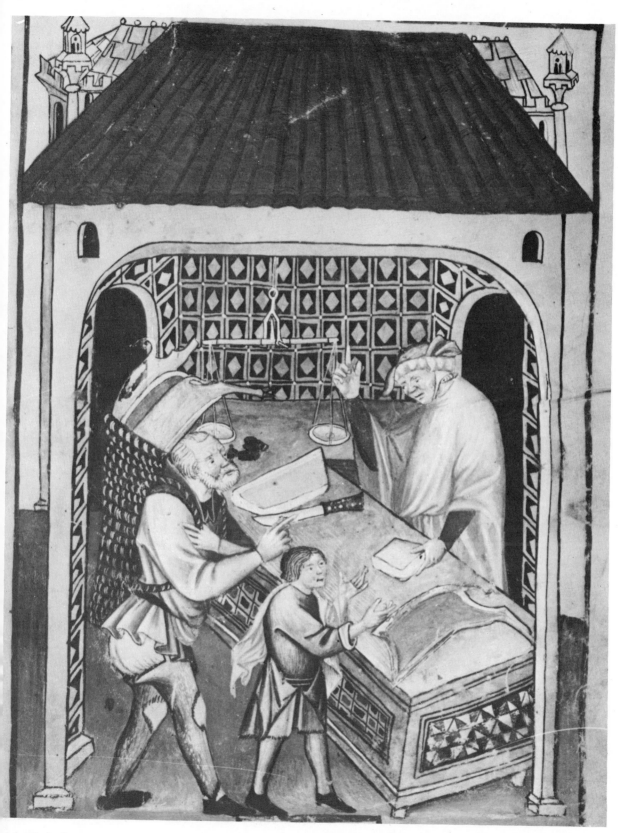

A butcher's shop

LIFE IN THE TOWNS 151

thousand English markets, at which craftsmen sold everyday goods needed regularly by their customers. For every article sold, however, the trader had to pay a tax to the town. This guaranteed that he would be protected from thieves and robbers. In 1361 the market tolls in Lincoln were 1d. on every horse, ½d. on every ox, and 2d. on a cart.

In the market square, all the meat traders grouped their stalls in one corner, all the clothiers in another, and so on. Occasionally a trader would be accused of a bad sale. One London butcher called John:

... found a certain dead pig thrown out near the ditch outside Aldgate in the suburb of London; this sow he then cut up and exposed its flesh for sale, cooked and raw, to a woman called Agnes and others. ... When this was told to the city council it was decided that the flesh and skin of the said pig should be taken, together with the said John, to the pillory on Cornhill, and that John should be placed in the pillory and the meat burnt beside him.

Some Salisbury tradesmen were guilty of similar offences:

John Penrose sold unwholesome red wine. He was condemned to drink a draught of the wine, and the rest was poured over his head.

John Strode put dust in his bread. When the crust was broken, there was no bread, only a string of cobwebs.

Alice Pegges sold loaves of bread which weighed 4/5 of an ounce too little.

Fairs

In addition to the weekly market, many larger towns also held an annual fair. At Lincoln there were two. The first, on the feast of St Botolph, lasted from the 17th to the 29th of June and the second, on the feast of St Hugh, lasted for a whole month after 17 November. The annual fair was a much larger and more colourful event than the weekly market. Merchants and traders came from far and near: Frenchmen sold wine; Spaniards brought steel blades for swords; German Hansards sold iron, copper and furs; Venetians brought silks, spices, gold and jewels from the East. English merchants traded corn, wool and cattle.

Often there were quarrels at these fairs. Two men might disagree over the price of, or payment for, an article or sometimes a trader was accused of selling poor quality foods. For all these cases a special court was held every day. It was called the 'Piepowder' Court, from the French words *pieds poudreux* (dusty feet) and gave quick settlement of cases for people from far away so they could be off to trade in the next fair.

The Jews

The Jews were descended from the people who lived in the Holy Land before the birth of Jesus Christ. They believed in one God, but they did not believe that Jesus Christ was the Son of God. Many came to England after the Norman Conquest, but because they would not take Christian vows, they could not hold land or join in a guild. Therefore, they lived in boroughs or castles, relying on the protection of the king. Although they lived as separate groups from the other townspeople they became

wealthy by lending money out at interest. They helped to pay for crusading armies and the building of castles or cathedrals throughout Europe. People who were punished with heavy fines in court often went to the Jews for the money. In return they paid interest of 2d. or sometimes 3d. a week for every pound borrowed. The king, however, benefited most from the Jews. In return for his protection, he took taxes from them and required them to pay even for the right to marry. When a Jew died all his money went to the Crown, although most of it was returned to his heirs.

The Jews were very unpopular in medieval Europe. In Lincoln, for

This drawing was by an unknown artist. It was done on a parchment roll kept by some Jews to list payments of people's debts. Perhaps the artist was idling away his time while waiting for payment.

The Jew's House, Lincoln

instance, houses were burnt and Jews were killed in 1219 and 1220. Henry III published the following laws in 1253:

The king has provided and decreed that . . . in their churches the Jews should worship in subdued tones, so that Christians hear it not . . . and that no Christian man or woman serve any Jew or Jewess, nor eat with them, nor dwell in their house. . . . And that every Jew wear on his breast a conspicuous badge. And that no Jew enter any church nor stay therein to the dishonour of Christ. And that no Jew be received in any town without the special licence of the king, save in those towns where Jews have been wont to dwell.

Town government

If they had received a borough charter from the king, the tradesmen of a town were responsible for managing their own affairs. They had to defend the town and keep the peace, especially at night when thieves and other criminals were abroad. They also had to keep the town safe from fire, manage the market and fairs, and possibly send members to Parliament. Perhaps most important of all, they looked after roads and bridges, keeping them repaired and safe from footpads and robbers.

To do these jobs most large towns had a mayor and town council, elected by the burgesses – who were usually the richer tradesmen. To organise this work the elected officials met at the guildhall, like the one at Lincoln. Each town was divided into wards and each ward chose an equal number of council members. Lincoln, for example, had four wards and three council members were chosen from each. In 1338 they were ordered by Edward III:

. . . to show such care in safeguarding the city . . . that no harm may come to anyone; for if it does the king will punish the mayor and his bailiffs severely.

In Hereford the town council set up a great bell in the centre of the town:

. . . to give warning to all men living within the city . . . and it ought not to ring unless it be for some terrible fire burning . . . or for any enemies drawing near unto the city. And when it rings, all men should come at once with their weapons.

Town amusements

Like most other things in the medieval town, entertainment was mostly organised by the guilds. On feast days they would form a procession in the morning with each guild wearing its distinctive dress or livery. This would be followed by church services and feasts. The afternoon would then be given over to games like ball, cock-fighting, bear-baiting and different sports like archery, running and wrestling. In London, the young men of the town played on the river:

They play a kind of naval warfare. A shield is firmly bound to a tree in midstream, and a small boat, swiftly impelled by oars and the current of the river, carries on its stern a youth armed with a lance with which to strike the shield. If he strikes the shield and keeps his footing, he has achieved his aim. But if he strikes the shield too firmly and the lance remains in his hand, then he

is thrown into the river. . . . There are, however, two other boats nearby with several youths on board to rescue the striker when he rises on the crest of the wave.

On important church festivals the guilds would perform cycles of miracle or mystery plays, with each guild taking its turn to present a part of the story.

How do we know?

Medieval merchants were the first laymen in the Middle Ages to learn to read and write. They wanted to send business letters, often to merchants in other countries, to arrange for the transport or sale of goods or raw materials like wool. Also the new universities of Europe were situated in the towns. From merchants, scholars and travellers we get descriptions of medieval towns, of the houses, the markets and fairs, and the people.

Most towns were royal boroughs with charters from the king. The statutes and regulations which they published to govern their affairs still survive in many instances. It seems that citizens were always anxious to control beggars but generally willing to give money to the genuine poor. However, the defence of the town and the danger of fire caused most concern – they are mentioned most frequently in surviving regulations.

We can discover the size of medieval towns from the extent of their walls and their wealth from the surviving buildings. Finds of gold coins give evidence of the many different traders who came to the annual fairs. Local mystery and miracle plays are dramatic evidence. Many are still performed today in cities like York. In the Middle Ages every town guild had its own play – those of the shepherds of Wakefield or the mariners of Hull, for example.

Officials like the town crier had important jobs to do. Today many of the ceremonies and costumes survive. However, they are largely for show and have little practical importance (like the dress and ceremonies connected with the mayor of a town or city).

Using the evidence: the Chester Cycle of plays

In the Middle Ages, the city of Chester, like other cities, was famous for its cycle of mystery and miracle plays. These plays probably originated in St Werburgh's Abbey, where they would be performed in Latin to tell the Bible story at Easter and Whitsun. Later they were acted outside

the church in the streets; they now told the same story to the ordinary people in English.

The twenty-five plays acted out the main Old and New Testament stories from Adam and Eve to the Crucifixion. They were performed in Whitsun week: nine on Monday, nine on Tuesday, and the remaining seven on Wednesday. These were holidays and there was a carnival atmosphere throughout the city.

Each play was acted on a large cart and the carts were pulled in turn around the streets of the city. Many spectators watched from the streets, the houses or the city walls.

(1) A high scaffold with two rooms, a higher and lower, upon four or six wheels. In the lower they dressed themselves, in the upper room they played, being all open on the top, that all beholders might hear and see them. The places where they played were in every street. They began first at the Abbey gates, and when the first pageant was played, it was wheeled to the High Cross before the mayor. And so every street had a pageant playing before men at any one time.

Each play was arranged by a guild of one of the trades. On the Tuesday the goldsmiths and masons played the *Murder of the Innocents*, while the previous day the vintners and dyers had done *King Herod*. They shared the same cart. Here is a list of some of the many expenses which each guild had to pay.

(2) *The carriage or scaffold*

Timber for the carriage	8s.	4d.
Wood to make wheels	3s.	4d.
Boards and timber	5s.	
Nails to dress the carriage		3½d.
Stewards for watching the carriage all night		8d.
Payment for an apple tree		6d.
Ropes, nails, pins and thread		10d.

Players rehearsed and selected

The first rehearse at John Huntington's house		6d.
Drink after the rehearse	1s.	6d.
3 old cheeses		4d.
To William Lutter (minstrel) at rehearse		4½d.
A crock of ale and two gallons	1s.	8d.
Money laid down, seeking players	1s.	4d.

Payment for the actors

To Synean	3s.	4d.
To the Angel		4d.
To Thomas Ellan		12d.
To the 3rd Doctor		12d.
Washing the curtains		4d.
2 chickens		6d.
Bacon on Tuesday morning for players breakfast	8s.	
Rent for the carriage house near to Greyfriar Lane		8d.

Props for the stage

For mending Hell's mouth	2d.
For keeping a fire at Hell's mouth	4d.
For setting the world of fire	5d.

Performing a miracle play

The play *Noah's Flood* was performed by the Dee boatmen. The play starts with Noah and his family on stage, building the Ark. 'Have donne you men and weomen all,' says Noah, 'hye you, leste this water fall, to worche this shippe ... as God has bedden us doe.' (*Stop what you're doing, everyone. Listen to this water falling. Hurry up and build this ship ... as God has ordered us to do.*)

Noah's son then shows his axe 'as sharpe as any in all thys towne'. However, one or two men in the audience might not agree with that and shout out at the actors! Audiences were not usually well-behaved at open-air performances and would even throw things at the stage if they thought the acting was bad.

As soon as the ship was built, Noah tries to persuade his wife to enter. She refuses.

(3)   ... not or I see more neede
       though thou stande all day and stare.
(*... not till I feel it's absolutely necessary, even though you spend all day trying to make me.*)

The men in the audience would laugh at Noah's reply.

(4)   Lorde, that weomen bene crabbed aye
       and none are meke I dare well saye.
       That is well seene by mee todaye
       In witnesse of you eychone.

(*Lord, women are always bad-tempered, and I dare add none are sweet tempered. That's been clearly shown to me today, in front of each of you here.*)

Eventually she is persuaded to join the boat, but only by her sons.

There was a serious purpose behind the plays, too, as they were one of the main ways in which the people learned their religious beliefs (see page 144). The actor playing God himself would speak to the audience, encouraging them to avoid sin.

(5) Manslaughter also aye yee shall flee,
    for that is not playsante unto mee.
    They that shedden blood, hee or shee,
    ought-where amongste mankynde,
    that blood fowle sheded shalbe
    and vengeance have, men shall see.
    Therefore beware all of yee,
    you fall not into that synne.

(You must always avoid killing people, because it gives me no pleasure. Any man or woman who spills a person's blood anywhere spills that blood sinfully and shall be cursed, as you should know. Therefore, all of you take care that you do not commit this sin.)

Questions and further work

1 Look again at Document 2. How much was spent on food and drink altogether? (Remember there were twelve old pence in a shilling and twenty shillings in a pound.)

2 Compare what the actors were paid with the other items in Document 2. Do you think they were well paid for their work? Who seems to have been the most important actor in the play?

3 Make a list of all the people who would be involved in the performances of the plays, as well as the actors. What were their tasks?

4 Miracle plays were performed on public holidays. How did they provide (a) excitement and (b) amusement for the townspeople? (Look particularly at Documents 2, 3 and 4.)

5 Based on Bible stories, these plays were acted in English not Latin. Why was this important? (Re-read the Using the evidence section in chapter 11 if you are not sure.)

6 Imagine you were a stage-hand for the Noah play. Describe the day when it was your play's turn to go round Chester. (A stage-hand would look after and help with all the things the actors needed like axes, rain effects, costumes.)

7 The guilds were very important in the towns. Under the following headings list the kinds of work they did or organised to make the towns better places to live in:
    Trade and work
    Government
    Entertainment
    Helping guild members in trouble.
Can you think of any disadvantages of having guilds?

13 The aristocracy and chivalry

The life of a baron

Imagine a long dark winter evening in the thirteenth century. Inside the castle, a large log fire crackles as it burns brightly in the grate. The hall is draughty but the fire gives warmth and light. The rest of the hall is lit by candles, which cast long, flickering shadows across the room.

The lord of the castle sits on a hard wooden chair near the fire. The floor under his feet is cold stone. He wears a surcoat on which his coat of arms is brightly embroidered. How would he spend the evening? Perhaps he would play chess or dice. Perhaps he would watch his court jester.

One baron gave his jester the following charter:

John, by the grace of God, etc. Know that we have given to William Piculf, our fool, the lands of Foule-Ossanne, to have and to hold for himself and heirs, on condition of doing henceforth annually for ourself the service of fool, as long as he live.

During the day there were other pleasures. Most barons and knights hunted foxes, deer and even wolves. They often carried a favourite falcon hooded on their wrists. The most popular entertainment, however, was the tournament with its crowds, its bright colours and its rough action.

A medieval feast

Below A wooden cupboard

Bottom left The tower of Warwick Castle

The barons of England were very important men, tenants-in-chief of the king. The king gave them their lands. In return they gave an oath of homage, and kneeling before him, they placed their hands in his and said: 'I become your man from this day onward of life and limb, and to you I shall be true and faithful.'

A baron might be an earl or duke. During the day he dressed in a long, sleeved, woollen or linen tunic with long thick cloth stockings. In battle, he wore a coat of mail, made of flat rings of iron, and his armour.

The baron's home was his castle, though by the fourteenth century many lived in fortified manor houses instead. In either case, the main living room was the hall, heated by a huge central fire, and with very simple wooden furniture. The baron's family lived privately in the solar, a small room off the main hall.

There were just two main meals each day. Dinner was at about eleven o'clock and supper about five. At both there was usually a wide choice of food. One banquet given in 1295 by an archbishop included 300 ling, 600 cod, seven barrels of salt salmon, forty fresh salmon, 14 000 red herrings, seven barrels of fresh herrings, 8000 whelks and 600 eels. A more usual diet included meat: pork, poultry and game. This was liberally spiced with vinegar, mustard or pepper, as it was often heavily salted to prevent it from going rotten.

Above The Great Hall at Penshurst Place in Kent

Left A medieval garderobe

Chivalry

Only rich men could afford to fight as mounted knights in war. Weapons, armour and a suitable horse were very expensive. The rules of chivalry laid down how knights should behave and the word 'chivalry' comes from the French for horseman, *chevalier*.

Not all knights followed the rules. Very many did, however, and becoming a knight was a serious step. Young men spent the night before the ceremony praying alone in church. The next day they received their swords and took vows to protect and defend the church in battle.

St Bernard, preaching the Second Crusade, said:

> The soldier of Christ carries a sword for a good reason: to punish the wicked and defend the good. If he kills the evildoer or the Infidel, the soldier is not a murderer but the servant of Christ.

St Bernard helped to found the Templars in 1118. They were an order of monks who were also knights and wore a pure white uniform with a blood red cross on the chest and back. Their aim was to protect the Holy Land from the Moslems.

> Their first rule of life is obedience. They live a simple life and they earn their bread by mending their clothes and armour. They hate chess and dice; they neither hunt nor hawk. They detest actors, mummers and jugglers as vanities and follies ... they have the meakness of monks and the bold courage of knights.

Another military order of monks, the Hospitallers, were formed in 1120, with similar aims (see pages 111–13).

Many kings wished to be surrounded by brave and just knights and founded 'orders of chivalry'. In England Edward III founded the Order

Lord Luttrell with his lady

The Knights of the Order of the Garter in procession with Her Majesty the Queen at Windsor Castle

of the Garter during the Hundred Years War. It consisted of the king and twenty-five of his best knights, 'the bravest men in the realm', and they swore to 'be courageous and, having undertaken a just war, stand valiantly and bravely until they finally conquer'.

Preparing a knight

Preparing a young nobleman to be a knight was a long and complicated process. Between the ages of seven and fourteen he would be sent to the home of a knight to live as a page. He learned to wrestle, fight, sing, dance and run errands there.

At the age of fourteen he would be sent for another seven years to a second knight as his squire. Here he served his apprenticeship, perhaps travelling abroad to support his master in battle, and would certainly learn all the military skills of knighthood.

When he was twenty-one he was ready to become a knight himself. First he was made pure. He was given a bath to wash away his sins then dressed in a white tunic. Over this was placed a red robe and these words were said: 'Remember that you must not hesitate to shed the last drop of your blood in the defence of Holy Church.' Finally he was covered in a black garment, to signify death, but with a white belt to signify purity.

Dressed like this the candidate was taken to church. There he spent the night alone kneeling at the altar and watching over his armour and weapons for at least ten hours. The following morning in another special ceremony he confessed his sins. His sword was blessed and he took the vows of chivalry: 'to fear God, serve the king, protect the weak and live honourably'. Then he was dressed in his full armour and knelt before the king. He received the accolade, a stroke on the shoulder with the flat side of the king's sword. In this way he finally became a knight. To show his bravery and generosity, he then took part in a tournament while his squire gave money to the poor.

Knights in combat

Tournaments

At tournaments knights practised the difficult arts of riding, tilting and sword fighting, usually before a large crowd. There were three types of contest: the joust, a battle between two knights with lance, sword or mace; the tourney between two sides of combatants using swords; and the wager of battle, a form of trial, where one knight, accused of a crime, would try to defend his honour by fighting his accuser (see page 99).

In peacetime the joust was fought with blunted lances. Knights rode their horses at each other trying to break the opponent's lance, knock him off his horse, or knock his helmet off. Umpires kept a score. Points were lost for wounding the opponent's horse or for striking an opponent when his back was turned.

Because his face was completely hidden by his helmet it was difficult to recognise a knight either in the tournament or on the battlefield. Each knight therefore had a coat of arms, a surcoat with an embroidered crest placed over his armour. The same device or crest was also painted on his shield. Richard the Lionheart's coat was described as:

A statue of King Arthur dressed in medieval armour. Describe his armour and weapons. The statue is in Innsbruck, Austria.

Three lions of fine gold, set on a red background, courant, fierce, haughty and cruel, to signify that the king is dreadful to his enemies . . . yet towards those who seek his friendship or submit to his power, his kindness is soon rekindled.

Even after nobles stopped wearing armour in battle they kept their crests as coats of arms.

Tournaments were always popular. Large crowds of people would gather to watch the action. Noble ladies filled the stands, together with the friends and families of the challenging knights. Tournaments usually lasted for four days, with two for the joust, one for the tourney, and one for archery competitions for the poorer people. The evenings were spent in dancing and feasting.

It was a common part of chivalry that women were well treated. A chivalrous knight ought always to be courteous and gentle, protecting his lady and fighting for her in tournaments. The lady of the knight who won a tournament presented him with his prize herself. She, in turn, tried to appear beautiful for him. The ideal woman was thought to have blue eyes, golden hair brushed in a long plait, a small mouth and beautiful hands. However, she was expected to run the estates of her lord if he were away at war and also to be skilled in embroidery, needlework and household management.

Weapons and armour

The illustration overleaf shows a knight in his armour. The main weapons knights used were the sword and the lance. The sword head, weighing about one-and-a-half kilos, was made of steel and often decorated with gold or silver designs. The hilt consisted of a cross-guard to protect the hand and the grip. The pommel, a round knob to balance the sword, often contained some relic from a saint such as a hair or a drop of blood. This was thought to give the knight God's help in battle. The shaft of the lance, sometimes over ten feet long, was made of ash or sycamore. Attached to the end was a square pennant or flag with the heraldic sign of the knight painted on it. Most knights also carried either a battle axe or a mace (a heavy spiked club with a metal head). The knight's shield, like the pennant, carried his sign and was usually large enough to serve as a stretcher to carry him from the battle if he were injured or killed. The most important part of his equipment was his well-armoured war-horse or destrier.

However, if thrown from his horse in battle, the knight, weighed down by armour, would find difficulty in rising. By the end of the Middle Ages knights had to be raised on to their destriers by large cranes!

Medieval weapons

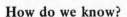

How do we know?

Much of the poetry of the Middle Ages was written to praise the virtue of the 'perfect gentle knight'. Chaucer's *Canterbury Tales* with its knight and squire tell us much. So do the romantic poems of the troubadours of France and even the writings of men like Richard the Lionheart. Froissart's *Chronicles* give a long account of the Hundred Years War fought between England and France. In them are many descriptions of the correct behaviour for knights in war.

But most important are the many remains of medieval castles, weapons and suits of armour still to be seen today.

Using the evidence: becoming a knight

The young nobleman served first as a page. A master was instructed to teach his pages:

(1) To ride cleanly and surely; to take them to jousts and teach them to harness their horses, and have courtesy in all their words and actions. . . . Moreover, to teach them sundry languages and other virtuous learnings, like harping, piping, singing and dancing.

It was especially important that the page learned to ride well, but he was also taught good manners:

(2) When you enter your lord's room, say, 'God's speed' and with humble cheer greet all who are there present. Do not rush in rudely but enter with your head up at an easy pace, and kneel on one knee to your lord.

If any speak to you at your coming, look straight at them with a steady eye and give good ear to their words while they be speaking and see to it with all your might that you chatter not.

Take no seat but be ready to stand until you are bidden to sit down. Do not scratch yourself or lean against any post in the presence of your lord.

Nor was religion forgotten. The page was instructed in the Christian virtues and the *Fourteen Works of Mercy*. It was a religious duty to feed the hungry, visit the sick and convert the sinner.

As a squire, the young noble taught himself to:

(3) Spring upon a horse armed at all points; to exercise himself in running, to strike for a length of time with an axe; to dance and do somersaults, fully-armed except for the helmet. Also to mount on horseback behind one of his comrades, by barely laying his hands on his sleeve; to mount a ladder placed against a tower, upon the reverse or underside, using his hands alone and without touching the rungs with his feet.

One young squire, called John, seems to have done exceptionally well:

(4) At the dinner he waited not just on his lady, but up and down throughout the hall; knight and lady, squire and page, groom and messenger, all he served according to their needs. . . . After dinner they washed their hands and went to play either in the forest or down by the river. John would often go to play in the Countess's chambers, teaching the ladies French or playing chess or dice.

Opposite A fifteenth-century gentleman pays court to his lady. He reads love poems to her while she sits and sews in her garden.

Perhaps the perfect squire was described by the poet Chaucer:

(5) Of his stature he was of even length
And wonderfully active, and great of strength.
He had been sometime in battle fray
In Flanders, Artois and in Picardy.
And borne him well, as of such little age. . . .
Short was his gown with sleeves long and wide
Well could he sit on horse and well ride
He could songs make and well endite,
Jouse and also dance, and well draw and write.

Questions and further work

1 Make a coloured drawing of *either* the scene at a tournament *or* the ceremony of knighthood. Read the chapter carefully and look closely at the illustrations to make sure that the scene is accurate.

2 List the skills which a young nobleman was expected to learn, first as a page, then as a squire.

3 Describe the ways in which the tasks of a squire differed from those of a page.

4 Documents 1–4 describe the most important parts of a young nobleman's education. What do they *not* mention which is important today?

5 Imagine you are a young squire training to be a knight. Write a description of a typical day in your training, expressing your pleasure in, and dislike of, some of the things you have to do.

6 List five differences between the life led by a knight and that led by a villein. Did the knight work as hard as the villein? Which would you rather have been? Give reasons for your choice.

7 Compare the account given by the documents of education in the Middle Ages with what you are taught today. Are there any similarities? What do you think the differences tell us about life in the Middle Ages? (Think about your answer to question 4 above.)

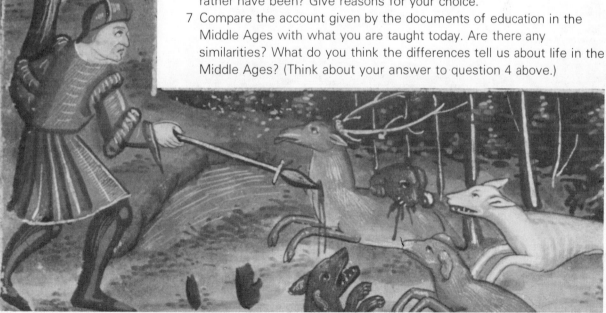

14

Monks and friars

The monastery at Rievaulx

In 1132 a saintly man called William arrived in England, with a dozen followers. They were sent from France by the famous St Bernard, the leader of the Cistercians or White Monks, to found a new monastery in Yorkshire. The monks set out to find a suitable place for their new home. They were fortunate and were given some land by a cheerful old knight called Walter Espec. One of them later described the place they chose:

The site was by one side of a rapid stream, called the Rie, in a broad-bottomed valley. . . . High hills, covered with many trees, surround the valley and give it privacy and beauty.

The place was perfect: lonely, beautiful, and with a good supply of water from the stream. All they needed now was stone to build their church. Luckily, higher up the stream, they found an outcrop of sandstone. They were able to float slabs of this stone downriver on rafts to the site of the building. Thus the Cistercian monastery at Rievaulx was founded.

Two years later, a Scottish nobleman called Ailred arrived at the monastery. He was an ambassador from King David of Scotland and he was advised by the Archbishop of York to visit Rievaulx. He did so and was much impressed by the 'life among friends' that he found. The next day he rode out from York intending to return to Scotland. His route took him over the hill just above the monastery. But as he rode past he thought he heard the bell of the church and felt he had to go down to see the monks again. He did so and stayed there for the rest of his life.

The nave of the abbey church at Rievaulx

Eventually he became abbot of the monastery and made Rievaulx one of the greatest medieval abbeys, with over 140 monks and 600 lay brothers.

Earlier monks and the Benedictine Rule

Long before the time of Ailred men had lived the life of monks. Some, for example, had lived and prayed to God as hermits in Egypt. One such hermit, St Symeon the Stylite, is said to have lived for thirty-three years on a small platform on top of two high pillars. His disciple, St Daniel, then tried to find peace alone in the same way. He stayed on his platform for thirty-three years and three months. The aim of these men was to cut themselves off from the noise of the world to worship God in peace.

Later, however, larger numbers of holy men began to live in communities or monasteries, where they would still be removed from the world, but where they could worship God together. One such group of monks was led by St Benedict of Nursia. He lived in Italy in the early years of the sixth century, when the land was invaded by barbarian Ostrogoths and torn by plagues and famine. As a result of these dangers, many men decided to leave their towns and seek safety in remote monasteries. Most of them were simple folk unlike the dedicated St Symeon or St Daniel, and therefore needed a 'rule for beginers', guiding them about the way they should live and the way they should worship God. In AD 529 St Benedict provided such a rule in his monastery at Monte Cassino.

His rules were simple. All monks must attend prayers or church services eight times each day, for a total of about five hours, and

'practise silence at all times especially at night'. They must take vows or promises to live pure and obedient lives, with no possessions of their own. There were also rules to cover the daily life. All monks must wear warm clothes and have enough sleep and food. All of them had to assist with the work, in the fields or the kitchen or elsewhere.

All the monks shall sleep in separate beds but, if it is possible, they shall all sleep in a common dormitory. . . . The younger brothers are not to have their

Black monks or Benedictines at mass

beds next to each other, but among those of the elders. Let the elders rouse the sleepyheads and help them to get up.... The brothers are so to serve each other that no one can be excused from the work of the kitchen. On Saturday, the monk who ends his weekly service must clear up everything.

The Benedictine Rule soon spread beyond Italy. The Black Monks (Benedictines wear black habits or robes) became famous throughout Europe. The first English Benedictine monastery was founded by St Augustine at Canterbury in AD 597 (see chapter 2).

The Cluniacs

Most monks after St Augustine's time were Benedictines, but they did not always keep the rules which St Benedict laid down. They failed particularly to go to the eight church services every day. But for four hundred years little was done to improve things.

Then William, Duke of Aquitaine, a French nobleman and a very devout man, gave his favourite piece of hunting land at Cluny to a group of monks to found a new monastery. Here a new kind of life was created. The monks spent most of their time in prayer and services in a beautiful marble church with fine coloured glass windows. They followed St Benedict's rules, strictly. They emphasised not work in the fields or the kitchen, but regular worship of God. So too did St Dunstan, who built up the magnificent abbey at Glastonbury in England in the same way.

The Cistercians

Perhaps the best attempt to keep strictly to St Benedict's rules in the Middle Ages was made by the Cistercians. It was to this group that Ailred of Rievaulx belonged. Their first monastery was founded in

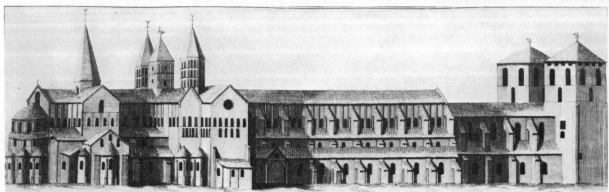

1098, in Citeaux in Burgundy, and one of the founders was an Englishman called Stephen Harding. He also wrote *The Charter of Love*, a special Cistercian version of the Benedictine Rule. Soon monks from Citeaux were being sent to found daughter-houses all over Europe and one of these monks was the William who became the first abbot of Rievaulx.

The monastic church at Cluny

Cistercian monks like those at Rievaulx lived a very hard life. Each day they had a full timetable of church services. They began in winter at 2 o'clock in the morning and ended after dusk in the evening. In between the services, they worked either in the fields or in the kitchen. Each morning there was a meeting or chapter, at which one section of the Benedictine Rule was read aloud. Work was allotted to monks for the coming day and punishments were given to those monks who had worked badly or fallen asleep in church.

In summer, the daily programme was slightly different because more time was needed in the fields, especially during harvest, when several of the services had to be said outside in the open air. During meals in the refectory, passages from the Bible were read and silence and proper table manners were to be observed. Monks were warned not to put their fingers in their cups or to wipe their knives on the table cloth. They lived on a simple vegetarian diet which consisted mostly of bread, together with cheese, fruit and vegetables. Fish, meat and eggs were not allowed.

Their afternoon work, therefore, was mainly to produce the food they ate. In 1132 the first house at Rievaulx was built on stony ground amid thick forest. Soon the monks had cleared a patch of timber and stones, ploughed it and sowed corn. Close to the monastery they started a vegetable garden. On the hillsides they reared sheep for the wool that they needed. Merchants were soon selling the surplus at local and even overseas markets.

In addition, of course, many men gave land to the monastery. Sometimes this land was so far from Rievaulx, that small 'granges' had to be built where monks could live and look after the sheep in the summer months.

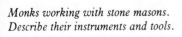

Monks working with stone masons. Describe their instruments and tools.

An aerial photograph of a Cistercian grange

Monks and lay-brothers

Soon many specialist workers were needed by the monastery, like blacksmiths, carpenters or bakers. When the monks themselves did not have the necessary skills, they employed lay-brothers to do these jobs. These men did not have the education of choir monks, but they made the same promises and attended some of the church services. From the plan of Rievaulx abbey you can see how many specialised jobs there were. A refectorer looked after the kitchen; an infirmarian the hospital and a cellarer the supply and storing of food. And there were many others as well.

The friars

When many monasteries became so large, they also became very rich from the profits of their surplus wool sales. According to their vows this was wrong; they were supposed to live in poverty.

By this time, many people were criticising the Church for other reasons too. One such man was the son of a rich Italian cloth merchant, John Bernadone, better known as St Francis of Assisi. When he was

Pope Innocent III receives St Francis in 1209

young, John was given plenty of money and lived a life of pleasure and gaiety with his friends in Assisi. Suddenly he changed. He abandoned all his money and went to the hills outside the town to pray. He was joined by a number of disciples but, unlike monks, they had no settled home. Instead, they wandered around the hills of Tuscany, doing good for the ordinary people. They helped with the harvest, nursed lepers, and taught simple folk how to pray. In return the people gave them food to eat and this satisfied their needs. Pope Innocent III officially approved the Franciscan order in 1209 and allowed them to wear a dark grey habit.

At the same time in Spain, a young nobleman called Dominic de Guzman had a similar idea. His main aim, however, was to preach to and teach the ordinary people, so that they could really understand about God. As a result of his work, the 'Friars Preacher' in their white habits were officially approved by the pope in 1216.

Both the Franciscans and the Dominicans helped the common people throughout Europe from the Baltic Sea to Africa. They looked after the sick and founded schools and hospitals. In 1245 a group of Franciscans was sent by the pope to the Great Khan of Tartary and in 1292 John of Monte Corvino founded a Franciscan church in China at Peking. John wrote this account in 1298:

I have baptised there at this time about 6000 Chinese persons. I have taught men and boys to read Latin, I have translated hymn-books and psalms. . . . The Emperor is said to be greatly delighted at their chanting.

The Pope, in response to John's letters, sent more friars to Peking and the church survived until 1362, when all Christians in China were murdered.

The later Middle Ages

However, people continued to criticise the Church. The fourteenth-century poet, Chaucer, described a monk who was keen on hunting, kept greyhounds, hated to work in the fields and spent most of his time away from his monastery. The following ten sins were condemned by one monastery, but were all too common in others:

> Thinking too much of comfort
> Being tempted by rich food
> Making too much noise
> Quarrelling in chapter meetings
> Being disorderly in church
> Being careless
> Being disobedient
> Being lazy
> Wanting your own way
> Thinking worldly thoughts.

Many people thought it a good idea, therefore, when Henry VIII closed the monasteries in England in 1539.

How do we know?

We know about the monks partly from the remains of their famous monasteries and partly from what they wrote about themselves. We have the rules which they wrote for their own lives, like the Benedictine Rule or the Cistercian *Charter of Love*. We also have descriptions written by monks about other monks, such as the one that Walter Daniel wrote about Ailred of Rievaulx (see Document 3, page 177). These are clearly biased in favour of the men they describe. Finally we have the descriptions of monks and friars written by ordinary men like the poet, Chaucer.

The monk in Chaucer's Canterbury Tales. *Chaucer made fun of him because he went hunting and kept dogs.*

A monk at work copying a manuscript

529	The Benedictine Rule	
910	The foundation of Cluny	Monks
1098	The foundation of Citeaux	
1132	The monastery at Rievaulx	
1209	The Franciscan Order	Friars
1216	The Dominican Order	
1536–9	Henry VIII closes the English monasteries	

Using the evidence: the White Monks

The first problem which the White Monks faced was the building of their monastery. In 1115 St Bernard left Citeaux with a group of followers and:

(1) They found a deep valley opening to the east. Thick forests gave it a gloomy character, but a flowing stream provided many advantages. In June they took up their abode in this valley and began to look for shelter against the approach of winter. His crude building consisted of a single roof under which a chapel, dormitory and refectory were all included. Neither stone nor wood concealed the bare earth floor. Windows no wider than a man's head admitted little light. In this room the monks took their frugal meals of herbs and water.

By September, Bernard's followers wanted to return to the comforts of Citeaux since they had no money to improve their monastery. St Bernard prayed for help and a passing stranger gave the monks £10 to buy shoes and food.

When the monastery at Clairvaux was established, a friend of St Bernard's visited the monks. He wrote this about them:

(2) I do believe they are the perfect followers of Christ in all things. They are clearly seen, by their quiet and gentle speech, to be God's companions; and when they openly praise God with psalms and hymns, their love and devotion are obvious. They even sing, without becoming tired, from before midnight to the dawn of the day, with only a brief interval. . . .
I see them, too, in the garden with hoes, in the meadows with rakes, in the fields with scythes, in the forests with axes. . . . I see men working in humility, men who were once bishops or earls.

Some of the monks definitely led a hard life. They ate very little and tried to punish their bodies by painfully whipping themselves or wearing hair shirts next to their skins. Ailred, the abbot of Rievaulx, was one of these and this account was written by one of his followers:

(3) He gave his frail body no pleasure at all in this earthly life. His bones could be clearly seen through his thin flesh and his lips seemed to frame his teeth. He ate scarcely anything and drank even less.

Not all monks were as devoted as Ailred or Bernard, but in some ways a group of White Monks called Carthusians were the strictest of all:

(4) The mountain of the Grand Chartreuse is very high and near the top is a deep, wild valley with many springs of water. Here Bruno and his followers built separate cells in which to live. Every Sunday Bruno gave each man vegetables to last for the week, but for three days each week they lived on bread and water alone. No one ever went from his cell, except to go to the church. All the time they spent reading and praying.

On the other hand many monks did not keep the rules strictly. One writer condemns those monks with bad table manners:

(5) Let nothing be done at table with great tumult or noise. . . . Some monks sit in one place, but their eyes and hands roam everywhere. They crumble bread, pour their wine and draw up their meat all at the same time. Others want different sorts of food and fancy seasonings.

Ailred and the White monks

Most sins of this kind were thought to be the work of the Devil.

(6) In church, devils make us sing badly. One day when the abbot's choir was singing the psalm on a low note, a certain young monk started singing five notes higher than anyone else. Some monks joined him, others stuck to the original, and some stopped singing altogether because of the dreadful noise. . . . Then the prior saw a devil coming out of the mouth of the young monk and he knew the cause of all the trouble.

St Guthlac receives the tonsure

Many monasteries at this time had young novices or boy-monks who were being trained into the life of the monastery. This rule was written for Benedictine novices:

(7) When a boy is offered to the monastery, let his parents bring him to the altar and wrap the boy's hand in the altar cloth. Then, having kissed it, let them put it into the hands of the monk who is receiving the boy and make the sign of the cross over his head. Then let the abbot cut the hair with shears around his neck.

In the dormitory, let the masters sleep between every two boys and sit between every two boys at other times. When they lie down in bed let a master always be near with a candle. . . . Their only punishment is to be whipped with a rod or have their hair stoutly pulled. Never should they be kicked or hit.

Questions and further work

1 List the main differences between a hermit, a monk and a friar. What did they have in common?
2 What were the different orders called? Under the name of each order list the colour of habit, whether they were monks or friars and as many of the order's rules as you can find in the chapter.
3 Who were the lay-brothers? List the kinds of jobs they did. Why do you think the monks employed them?
4 Join together with other members of your class to write a project on medieval monks. You should try to answer the question: 'How did monks live in the Middle Ages?'. Use the material in this chapter, including the pictures and the documents to help you.

A monastic school

Here are some suggestions for sections. You may have more.
In what places did they settle?
What were their buildings like?
How did they organise their day?
What jobs did they do?
What food did they eat?
Do you think Document 2 tells the truth about Cistercian monks?
Does Document 5?
How did they worship God?
5 Why did people begin to criticise the monks and later the friars towards the end of the Middle Ages?

15

Life at school and university

A student riot

The following account comes from the Oxford Coroner's Roll for 1314. It shows that student riots and teenage violence were just as common in the Middle Ages as they are today:

The jury say upon their oath that on the Saturday aforesaid, after the hour of noon, the northern students on the one part, and the southern and Welsh students on the other part came to St John's Street and Grope Lane with swords, bucklers, bows, arrows and other arms and there they fought together. And in the conflict Robert de Bridlington and other men stood together in a certain upper chamber in Gutter Hall, situated in St John's Street, shooting

A university beadle, the official responsible for keeping students in order

arrows down through a window into Grope Lane. And there the said Robert de Bridlington, with a small arrow, smote Henry of Holy Isle and wounded him hard by the throat on the left side; and the wound went even unto the heart; and thus he slew him. Moreover the jury say that the other men encouraged the said Robert to shoot Henry dead.

The story is typical of a number of incidents at fourteenth-century Oxford. In a 'great slaughter' in 1354, thirty-nine men were identified as having killed men of the other side, but of these only one or two were hanged, the rest escaping or fleeing to the sanctuary of a church.

Such violence was partly the result of the hard life lived by students. Studies were often dull, rules were always strict.

The schools

In medieval England most people were illiterate. There was little chance for children to go to school. Parents had to teach their own children the first stages of reading and writing, though occasionally an elder brother or a local priest might be willing to help. Some churches

had 'song schools' where choirboys could learn to sing. First they had to learn to read and a few other parents would ask the priest to take their children into the reading classes. In such schools, children learned nothing beyond reading a few simple words and reciting the Lord's Prayer and the Creed.

It was in grammar schools that medieval boys received a good basic education. These were usually founded in towns or villages by rich landowners or merchants. The aristocracy did not need them because the sons of noblemen were taught elsewhere as pages and squires, and ordinary people were too poor to be able to send their children to them.

In grammar schools boys were taught to read and write Latin grammar, since Latin was the common language of educated men throughout Europe. Priests conducted services, scholars wrote books and merchants kept their records in Latin. There were two Latin textbooks, Priscian's *Grammar* and Donatus' *Ars Minor* but only the teacher had a copy. He stood at the front of the class and dictated a sentence or two from the book. The class then recited the sentence until it was learnt by heart. The pupil who mastered the grammar could go on to learn to read easy passages from Aesop's *Fables* or the Latin poets or the Bible.

Life at one of these schools was certainly much less pleasant that it is at school today. The pupils had to stand or sit for eight or nine hours reciting Latin sentences, which they sometimes failed to understand. Older boys would be required to make speeches or debate in Latin. In some schools even private conversations had to be conducted in Latin. If any pupil made a mistake in his reciting he was beaten with the rod. One lady encouraged her son's teacher to 'trewly belassch hym tyl he wyll amend'. Games were forbidden in schools, except on the few feast days or Saints' Days which were holidays for everyone.

By the fifteenth century there were grammar schools in most towns: London have five, Bristol, Norwich and York two or three each. In 1440 Henry VI founded a school at Eton for four clerks, six choristers and twenty-five pupils. Most schools, however, had just one room, one master and perhaps twenty boys at different stages of their education. The master had the impossible task of teaching all the pupils together!

The were other schools which taught grammar too. Many rich men

The Norman staircase at the King's School, Canterbury

left money in their wills to found charities where a priest would be kept to pray for the souls of the man and his family. In addition the priest was often required to teach local children basic Latin grammar. There were about two thousand such schools in England, though some of them taught but a few children. Cathedral schools, on the other hand, like those at Durham and Canterbury, were among the best in the land. The teachers in these schools, and in one or two monastery schools, were learned monks. They sometimes also taught intelligent pupils from poor homes.

The universities

Once a young man had learned to read and write and understood the basic rules of grammar, he could go to study at a university. There were three main types of university in Europe. Medicine was studied in the south of Europe, at Salerno in Sicily and Montpellier in France. To study law a student would go to Italy, especially to the University of Bologna. But if he wanted to study religion or philosophy he would have to go to Paris or Oxford.

It was at Oxford that the first major English university grew up, probably in the reign of Henry II. When Henry quarrelled with his friend, Thomas Becket, the Archbishop of Canterbury, Becket fled overseas to France. Many young English scholars went with him and began to study at Paris. When Becket was murdered, Henry ordered all these students to return home and they gathered at Oxford to continue their studies.

A number of teachers formed themselves into a guild of masters and soon scholars were coming from all over Europe to hear their lectures. Then in 1209 a quarrel took place between the students and the townsmen at Oxford and many students and some masters left the city. They went to a little village in East Anglia and decided to set up a second university. This was the beginning of the University of Cambridge.

In Paris, Oxford and Cambridge, the guild of masters began the idea of providing a number of houses in the town where their students could live at a low rent and under supervision. There were four or five students to each room, often two or three to a bed, and meals were eaten by all in the house dining room. This was a good idea, but even so some very poor students could not afford the rent. They lived in small attics, badly-fed and half-frozen, until some wealthy people began to give money to build colleges where poor scholars could live free of charge. In 1257 Robert of Sorbon, the chaplain of Louis IX of France, founded a college in Paris for poor scholars. Today the Sorbonne is one of the greatest universities in France. Such colleges soon developed into places where masters arranged discussions and lectures for students.

Degrees

At any one time there were probably about a thousand students at Oxford but life was uncomfortable and their studies were hard. To reach the first degree, the Bachelor of Arts, a student had to attend lectures for eighteen months or two years and then take a verbal examination before one of the masters. If he passed this, he could then do some teaching in the University. He then had to study for possibly a further six years before he became a Master of Arts.

All lectures were given in Latin and, like certain schools, some colleges even warned their students that private conversation should also be conducted in Latin. The main problem for the student was how to get books. Each college had a library with a number of books chained to the wall so that they could not be stolen. In addition each university had a number of 'stationers' who were required to rent out books to students at a fixed price. Each book had to be copied out by hand, illuminated beautifully in the margins, corrected by another copyist and then bound in leather. Before the invention of printing in the fifteenth century this was a long and costly business.

It is not surprising that very few students passed their exams. At Oxford only eighty students a year became either BA or MA while at Cambridge the number rarely exceeded fifty.

The course for the Bachelor of Arts degree was in two parts. The first part, the *trivium* as it was called, was in three sections: grammar, rhetoric and logic; the second part, the *quadrivium*, had four: astronomy, arithmetic, music and geometry. As you will see later, there was very little work in science in the Middle Ages.

Student life

At both Oxford and Cambridge a student would live in a student's house or hall or sometimes in a college. The student's day would start early, perhaps about 6 a.m. in the summer. Because candles were expensive in the Middle Ages, the hours of daylight were used to the full. The student would perhaps wash along with other students in an open trough in the middle of the college. He would probably have no breakfast and attend lectures from 6 a.m. until 10 a.m. which was the usual time for dinner. Lectures began again at 1 p.m. and continued until 5 p.m. which was supper time. After supper masters and students were expected to devote their time to private work until 8 or 9 p.m. when most people went to bed.

Life was certainly uncomfortable. The poor scholar would have little money for food and clothing. The lecture halls were little more than sheds where masters and pupils sat on straw on the floor. In Paris the street where the schools were situated was called Straw Street. It must have been terribly cold to wash in an icy trough on a cold winter's morning and then trudge through the snow for four hours of lectures in a draughty shed!

In spite of its hardships, life was expensive. Here is a letter from one French student to his father:

Dear father,
I have not a penny and I have no hope of getting any except through you, for all things at the university are so dear. Nor can I study in my law books, for they are all tattered. I owe ten crowns in dues to the Provost and you are my last hope.

A school in Italy. The books are chained to the benches.

Some students, however, got other debts:

Dear father,
To ease my debts contracted at the tavern, at the baker's, the barber's, the laundry and the doctor's, I send you greetings and a request for money.

Discipline

Many students, though, were wealthy enough to enjoy their life at university and the masters found it difficult to discipline them. The rod or birch cane were not used in medieval universities. The most common method of punishment was the fine. You can see what many students got up to from the following law from a university in Germany:

None of you shall presume to join fencing classes or practise fencing under penalty of two florins.
    None of you shall go around after the ringing of the bell without a light, or with your light hidden in the sleeve of your cloak, or with your face covered or masked, under penalty of one florin.
    None of you shall climb on the city walls at night, or attack the townsmen or knock down bridges, under penalty of one florin.

The rules of King's College, Cambridge, were also severe:

No scholar, fellow or servant of the college shall keep dogs, hunting or fishing nets. Nor shall they have within the college any ape, bear, fox or badger or any other strange beast. We forbid the games of dice, ball and chess as dishonest sports which may involve gambling, especially in the college chapel and hall.

The colleges also had to have rules for the daily routine. These were written by Robert of Sorbon:

If a student is late for dinner, he shall be given his full portion if he comes from lectures, but he shall be given only bread if he has been on his own affairs.
    No woman shall eat with students in their rooms. Also no student shall bring friends frequently to eat or drink at the expense of the College.
    No student shall have the keys of the kitchen.

In spite of all the hardships and rules, life at the university may not have been so unpleasant. Sunday was a day of rest and all holy days, about fifty a year, were days for games, merrymaking and enjoyment.

This carving of students at school comes from Notre Dame in Paris

Using the evidence: medical teaching

Western Europe in the later Middle Ages knew very little about the workings of the human body or the prevention and cure of illnesses. Doctors thought that all matter in the body was made up of four 'humours' in very precise quantities: blood, phlegm, black bile and yellow bile. Illness occurred when one of the humours expanded and overflowed. The following account by a very learned and respected thirteenth-century doctor is typical:

(1) In olden days women were exceedingly temperate, eating and drinking but little, yet now is gluttony become an ingrained custom with them. . . . Right in the midst of thy body lieth a stomach that receiveth whatsoever thou eatest or drinkest; and the same stomach is shaped like a cauldron on the fire, wherein

Quodam qq; tpre du sciffim gregis dnici
paftor sua luftrando circuiret ouilia.
deuenit inmontana & agreftia loca ubi

we boil our food. Ye see well how if the cauldron on the fire be filled too full, then must one of two evil things come to pass. Either the cauldron will boil over ... or the food must burn in the cauldron, but if a man fill the cauldron in all temperance, then the food may be well sodden and find room to simmer quietly through and through.... The liver lieth hard by the stomach like a fire, for the liver hath by nature the greatest heat of the whole body and bringeth heat to the cauldron of the stomach.

It was hardly surprising that knowledge was so limited, since the church discouraged surgery and forbade dissection – that is, the cutting up of the bodies of the dead. Some surgeons did defy the ban. During a plague in Italy in 1286, a Franciscan monk opened a corpse to see if he could discover the cause of the disease. By the beginning of the fourteenth century post mortem examinations were not uncommon at Oxford. But even as late as the fifteenth century university lecturers in medicine rarely examined bodies themselves.

Often the advice which doctors gave their patients was wrong:

(2) Against toothache. Take a candle of mutton fat and burn it as close as possible to the tooth, holding a basin of cold water beneath it. The worms which are gnawing the tooth will fall into the water to escape the heat of the candle.

And only rarely did the doctors themselves get good advice:

(3) The doctor should also have clean hands and well-sharpened nails and be cleansed of all blackness and filth. And be he courteous at his lord's table and not offend the guests sitting by him in words or deeds.... Also let him have a store of good honest tales that may make his patients laugh.

In the medieval world, only the Moslems had an advanced knowledge of medicine. A doctor called Rhazes wrote many books including *On Smallpox and Measles*:

A doctor helps one patient to inhale and advises the other about his measles

Two Arab doctors examine a patient

(4) The outbreak of smallpox is preceded by continuous fever, aching in the back and shivering during sleep. The main symptoms of its presence are: backache, fever, stinging pains, violent redness of cheeks and eyes and a difficulty of breathing and coughing. . . . Excitement, nausea and unrest are more pronounced in measles than they are in smallpox, while the aching in the back is more severe in smallpox.

Another of the many Moslem medical books was *On Plague*:

(5) The spread of disease is established by study, through the senses, of garments, vessels, even ear-rings; by the spread of it by persons from one house to another. . . . The result of my long experience is that if a person comes into contact with a patient, he is immediately attacked by the same symptoms.

Questions and further work

1 Draw a picture of a lecture hall where a medical lecture is being given. Read the chapter carefully and look at the illustrations to make sure your drawing is accurate.

2 Read the description of the stomach in Document 1. What does the lecturer describe the stomach as being like? What do you think would happen to the patient if the stomach 'will boil over' or if 'the food must burn' after he has eaten something?

3 Write out the following statements. Against each, say whether it is true or false and give evidence from the documents for your view.
(a) Medieval doctors in western Europe had little first-hand knowledge of the workings of the human body.
(b) Moslem medicine was much more scientific than that of the West.

4 Documents 3 and 4 both give advice to doctors. What advice does each give? What does it tell you of the man who wrote it? Do you think the advice in each document is still useful today?

5 Imagine you are a student who has just started at Oxford University in the fourteenth century. Write a letter to your father, telling him of your life at Oxford and how it is different from your school days.

The later Middle Ages

16 Kings and people

King John

Runnymede is a small island in the river Thames, west of London. On a summer day in June 1215 the island and the banks alongside the river were alive with the noise and bustle of hundreds of people. Among the many tents one stood clear of the rest. Four horses, still hot with sweat, stamped and snorted in the clearing nearby.

Inside the tent the voices were loud and angry. The Earl of Winchester and Robert Fitzwalter, a baron from East Anglia, were shouting at their king. John was King of England and Lord of Ireland, but they said they were tired of his bad government. Eustace de Vesci, sly and cunning, said little. The two other men in the tent, Archbishop Stephen of Canterbury and William the Marshal, were for the moment also quiet.

The barons had given the king a document. Called the 'Articles of the Barons', it contained a list of grievances. They said he had collected unfair taxes, taken hostages from them and asked them to fight in foreign wars. Many barons had joined their army. They would make war on the king if he didn't listen.

John too was angry. How dare these upstarts criticise him? He was their king; they had no right to question him. He swore abuse at his visitors.

'My Lord!' the Archbishop cried as he tried to cool things down. But in the end John saw he was trapped. The barons' army was too big and he would have to give way. William Marshall said it would be better to sit down calmly and talk things over. Perhaps the Earl of Winchester would recite a list of grievances.

They talked late into the night. At times the king became angry again. But peace was kept. Next day more barons joined the discussion and within a week they had what they wanted. John put his seal to Magna Carta, a charter of liberties or freedoms for Englishmen. In solemn ceremony he gave the kiss of peace on both cheeks to the barons' leaders and vowed to keep the promises he made in the charter.

Later medieval kings

For the next three hundred years King John's successors faced similar

Henry V

Henry VI

problems. They were always short of money to fight wars in France or against the Welsh or Scots. Many of them found it difficult to keep control of their barons.

Richard III (1483–5)

Edward IV was a strong and healthy man. Yet in April 1483, suddenly and unexpectedly he felt violent pains in his stomach. It may have been a burst appendix. After an illness of only ten days he died.

He had two sons: Edward, Prince of Wales, who was twelve years old and Richard, Duke of York, who was ten. Their uncle, Richard of Gloucester, became regent to look after the kingdom until Edward was old enough to rule. A coronation was fixed for 22 June and in May the two boys were seen playing together in the garden of the Tower of London.

But the coronation did not take place and the boys were never seen again. Instead Richard of Gloucester agreed to a request from

Richard III

Parliament and proclaimed himself as Richard III. Richard then accused some of his enemies in the Royal Council of treason. Lord Hastings was seized by the king's guards. Using a log as a base they cut of his head with a sword – at least according to popular story. Many other people were arrested, too, all over the country.

Afterwards, however, Richard III was supposed to be full of guilt. In Shakespeare's play he appears as a cruel hunchback filled with shame.

> ... Alas, I rather hate myself
> For hateful deeds committed by myself.
> I am a villain.

Two years later, after another civil war, he was killed on the battlefield at Bosworth.

The power of Parliament

Parliament in the Middle Ages was very different from that of today. At first, bishops and barons assembled at the king's invitation to approve his policy. The king called a Parliament as and where he chose, and invited only those people he wanted to attend.

By the thirteenth century, however, certain procedures were usually followed and the influence of Parliament increased. In 1295 Edward I also invited two representatives from each county and two from some of the boroughs. This had been done once before by the rebel, Simon de Montfort. Edward's action marked a permanent change, though, and recognition of the importance of the towns. People other than a small number of barons began to play a part in governing the country.

The seal of Simon de Montfort

Two separate houses of Parliament, Lords and Commons, later developed. The Commons became specifically concerned with petitions to the king whenever his policies were harmful to the 'common interest'. By the mid-fourteenth century it was recognised that all laws were made by the king and Parliament and that no laws could be changed without Parliament's approval.

In 1295 Edward I was desperate for money. The French had landed at Dover; the Welsh had rebelled and war had begun with the Scots. Edward summoned Parliament and demanded extra taxes, but they replied that 'that which touches all should be approved by all'. Edward III faced the same problem when fighting his expensive wars in France. But as well as large amounts of regular money, the king also needed the support of the gentry (the members of Parliament) to get local soldiers into his armies. Edward I and Edward III were both therefore forced to give privileges to Parliament to secure support for their policies.

Later in the fourteenth century Parliament was asked to support the barons against Richard II; Parliament approved the execution of some of Richard's ministers and strengthened their own claim to help choose the king's advisers. In addition many medieval kings died suddenly or were killed in battle. Their successors always sought the approval of Parliament before they finally took the throne, and this further increased the importance of the assembly.

How do we know?

Medieval kings have left us more written information about their activities than have medieval peasants. We have chronicles such as the one written by Holinshed, the source used by William Shakespeare in writing his history plays about Richard II, Richard III, Henry IV, Henry V and Henry VI. We also possess the evidence of records, the letters and documents of government departments, especially those of the Chancery, the king's writing office. Perhaps the best sources, however, are the letters written by important private individuals in this period. The Stonor and Paston letters (see page 143) and the Cely papers all provide information useful to the historian.

The Black Death (1348–9)

In the summer of 1346 men in western Europe heard stories of terrible disasters in eastern countries:

St Stephen's Hall at Westminster

A session of Parliament. Try to identify the different people and groups in the picture.

Between China and Persia there rained a vast rain of fire falling in flakes like snow and burning up mountains and plains and other lands with men and women; and then arose vast masses of smoke, and whosoever saw it died within half a day; and likewise any man or woman who looked upon those who saw it.

This was the plague. It had terrible effects:

India was depopulated, Persia, Syria and Asia Minor were littered with dead bodies . . . none were left alive.

In the Black Sea the Genoese had a trading station. One day a Genoese trader killed a local man in a brawl and the local people, the Tartars, attacked the merchants. They fled inside their castle, but while they were besieged the plague spread among the Tartar army. Many died in agony. However, before the siege was ended, the Tartars used giant catapults to lob corpses into the castle. As a result the plague spread among the Genoese, who quickly took to their ships and sailed home.

In January 1348 three galleys arrived in Genoa, driven by a fierce wind from the east, horribly infected with plague. When the people of Genoa saw that the disease was on board, they drove off the sailors by firing burning arrows. . . . Thus the ships were scattered from port to port, carrying the disease wherever they went.

From Italy the disease spread rapidly throughout Europe and to England. The first sign of the disease was 'the emergence of small lumps

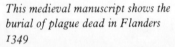
This medieval manuscript shows the burial of plague dead in Flanders 1349

in the groin or under the armpits, some of which were as large as a common apple'. Then black or red spots appeared and sores opened. The result was usually death.

The cause of the disease was a tiny germ called the *Pasteurella Pestis* which lived in the stomach of the flea. The flea in turn lived in the hair of a black rat and the rats of central Asia and the Near East were brought back to Europe in the ships of traders like the Genoese merchants mentioned above.

We have already seen what conditions were like in a medieval town: narrow and crowded streets, cramped and dirty houses, with no sanitation and only a common drain down the middle of each street. The disease spread to English towns in September 1348 and the worst period was probably the summer of 1349. It was so bad in London that new churchyards were consecrated and an inscription in one read:

A great plague raging in the year 1349, this churchyard was consecrated; wherein were buried more than fifty thousand bodies of the dead, whose souls God have mercy upon. Amen.

One French writer said that:

It is almost impossible to credit the mortality throughout the whole country. Travellers, merchants, pilgrims and others who have passed through it declare that they have found cattle wandering without herdsmen in the fields, towns and wasteland.... And in many areas both lands and fields are lying uncultivated.

The effects of the Black Death

The population of England in 1340 was probably about four million. How many of these were killed by the plague of 1348–9? One chronicler recorded that 'only one in ten survived'; another stated that 'three-quarters perished'. Because of the lack of evidence, it is difficult to know precisely how many died. These chroniclers probably exaggerated, and the epidemic killed perhaps one-third of the population. The proportion of priests killed, however, was higher: 49 per cent of all priests in the diocese of Winchester, Exeter and Norwich died and 39 per cent of those in the province of York. All told perhaps 45 per cent of English priests died. Why do you think the number was so high? It may have been because the parish priests were the men who gave the last sacrament to the dying and tended the sick during times of illness. However, 44 per cent of all English monks were killed by the plague and they did little of this sort of work. Bishops, of course, found it hard to replace so many dead priests and many parishes were left untended for some years after the Black Death.

In Europe, too, very many people died, perhaps one person in three overall. Some areas like Tuscany in central Italy suffered very heavy casualties; others like Bohemia in central Europe were hardly affected at all. Certainly more people died in the towns than in the rural areas. Here is Boccaccio's account of the effects on Tuscany:

Poor labourers and husbandmen with their whole families died most miserably

in out-houses, even in the open fields without any assistance from servants or doctors. . . . Men became lazy and slothful in their daily work, not minding their affairs but waiting for death every hour and forgetting their cattle, the fruits of the earth and their usual labours. Whereupon their oxen, asses, sheep and goats, the swine, poultry and their very dogs, being banished from their houses, went wildly wandering abroad the fields, where the corn still grew on the ground without being reaped or cut.

In what ways would farming suffer from such a catastrophe?

In England a number of villages were abandoned because many inhabitants died and the others fled. William of Dene, a monk from Rochester, records the effect on the land in Kent:

There was such a shortage of labourers and workmen that more than a third of the land in the whole realm was left to lie idle. . . . In every manor in Rochester buildings fell into decay and there was no manor which returned an income of £100.

For those labourers who survived the plague, however, life was much better. Most took over extra land, formerly held by men who had died. On the estates of Crowland Abbey, for instance, eighty-eight holdings were left empty but seventy-nine of these were quickly taken up by labourers from other parts of the estates. In addition wages rose considerably for those workers who were left. The ploughman at the manor of Cuxham near Oxford, for instance, saw his wage increase from 2s. a week to 10s. 6d. a week as a result of the Black Death.

If the labourer benefited from the Black Death, the landowner suffered. He had to pay higher wages for his labourers and much of his land was untilled. To add to this the price of his produce fell, thus giving him less profit. An oxen which fetched 13s. 7d. in 1347 was sold for 6s. 8d. in 1349 and a cow, formerly 9s., fell to 6s. 6d. The price of wool reached its lowest point for the whole fourteenth century, but the cost of corn remained steady because of the poor harvest in 1349. The landowner also suffered because the price of other goods increased as a result of plague. Salt, necessary for winter meat, and iron to make ploughs and other tools were obvious examples of this.

The Black Death, therefore, benefited the labourer rather than the landowner. The Statute of Labourers, passed by Parliament in 1351, decreed that no worker was to move from one area to another. That it was necessary to state this shows how much the labourers had benefited from the events of 1349. Men were in short supply and some land-owners paid high wages to persuade labourers to work for them.

Many people in Europe saw the Black Death as God's punishment for their sins. A small minority went to extremes trying to put things right. One group started the Flagellant movement. This probably originated in Hungary, then spread to Germany and the west. Usually two or three hundred people would march in a long procession, two by two, with men in the front and women in the rear. When they arrived in a town, they headed for the market place, pursued by many local people, and formed a huge circle.

Then they stripped to the waist and at a signal from their Master threw themselves to the ground. The Master moved among the Brethren with a whip and scourged their backs and chests: the whip usually had three or four leather thongs tipped with metal studs. Then each Brother took his own scourge, as one witness recounts:

With such scourges they lashed themselves on their naked bodies so that they became swollen and blue, the blood ran down to the ground and bespattered the walls. Occasionally they drove the spikes so deep into their flesh that they could only be removed by a second wrench.

The remarkable thing is that this ordeal lasted, twice or thrice a day, for thirty-three days as the Flagellants marched from town to town. Not all their sessions could have been as bloody as the one witnessed above. With no antiseptics and little hygiene, the Brethren would have died long before the thirty-three days were up.

The Peasants' Revolt (1381)

In May 1381 a tax collector called John Bampton was sent by the King to Fobbing in Essex to check on people who had refused to pay the King's Poll Tax. The townsmen told Bampton that 'they would have nothing to do with him nor give him one penny' and expelled him from the town. The King then sent some soldiers in but, by the time they arrived on 2 June, the men of Fobbing had been joined by other men of East Anglia and the soldiers were successfully driven out.

Kent and Essex now became alive with revolt. The Kent rebels attacked Dartford on 4 June. Rochester fell on the 6th and Maidstone on the 7th: here they chose as their leader Wat Tyler, a capable general who was called by one writer, 'the greatest robber in all Kent'. Under his leadership they pillaged the archbishop's palace at Canterbury and then marched towards London to Blackheath. At the same time the Essex rebels reached Mile End.

Meanwhile in London the fourteen-year-old King, Richard II, and Archbishop Sudbury of Canterbury had taken no defensive measures. On 13 June some London citizens who supported the rebels, allowed Tyler's army to enter the city by London Bridge; the Essex army

King Richard II talking to the rebels from a barge on the River Thames

The death of Wat Tyler

entered similarly by Aldgate. Both armies converged on the palace of John of Gaunt and ransacked it.

Tyler insisted there should be no looting. One man who stole a silver goblet was hung by the rebels. The King fled to the Tower to defend himself and there agreed to go the following day to Mile End to meet the Essex rebels. At this meeting they asked for the abolition of serfdom and the King agreed, so the men of Essex then began to go home.

However, while the king was at Mile End, Wat Tyler's men broke into the Tower, dragged out Sudbury, beheaded him and placed his head on London Bridge. This started a whole series of massacres in the capital particularly of foreign merchants and workers. The King could only hide for the night amid the terrible slaughter. On the next day he agreed to meet Tyler at Smithfield and the latter rode out with one companion to meet the King and present the grievances of the men of Kent. During the discussions Tyler asked for a drink and when he had drunk it his hand fell back and touched his sword. The Mayor of London, thinking that the rebel leader intended to kill the king, cut him down immediately. As soon as they saw this the rebels took up their arms, but the story goes that Richard bravely spurred his horse towards them and cried:

Sirs, will you shoot your king? I shall be your chief and captain, and you shall have from me what you seek. Only follow me to the fields outside the city.

The King's bravery ended the revolt and by nightfall most of the rebels were making their way home under royal escort. Gradually other riots, which had occurred all over the south of England, died out. In December 1381 the King published a pardon from which only a few individuals were excluded. The only real benefit which the rebels gained from the King, though, was the ending of the poll tax which had started off the revolt.

Using the evidence:
Why was there a Peasants' Revolt?

During and after 1381 many men asked who was to blame for the Peasants' Revolt. The three main views are expressed in the following three passages. The first is from a poem written probably in either 1381 or 1382; the second comes from the *History* of Thomas Walsingham, a monk of St Albans abbey; the third from the historian Froissart:

(1) The Rysing of the Comuynes in Ionde,
   The Pestilens and the earthe-quake –
   These three thinges, I understonde,
   Be-tokenes the grete vengaunce and wrake
   That shulde falle for synnes sake.

[handwritten: cos of sins people's]

(2) Many held the negligence of the Archbishop and his provincial bishops responsible, for in their care lies the faith and stability of the Christian religion. Certainly they allowed John Wycliffe and his followers to behave shamefully . . . and put their preaching about the whole country to corrupt the people. . . .

It seems to me that these evil times are the result of the sins of the people of the earth, especially the friars. Nowadays there is a saying 'This is a friar, and therefore a liar'.

[handwritten: cos of sin but espec. friars + negligence of bishops]

(3) There was a usage in England that the noblemen have great franchise over the commons and keep them in servage, that is to say, their tenants ought by custom to labour the lord's lands, to gather and bring home their corns, to make hay. . .and hew their wood. . . .

A priest of the county of Kent called John Ball used to preach to the people as they came from Mass on Sundays:

'My friends, the state of England cannot be right until everything is held in common and there is no difference between noblemen and serf and we are all as one. Why do nobles lord it over us?. . . . We are all descended from our first parents Adam and Eve, so how can they be better men than us?'

[handwritten: cos of feudal system]

Who do these three authors blame for the revolt? The following extracts indicate some other reasons for it. One of the vital factors was the Poll Tax of 1379:

(4) In the year 1379 King Richard II held his Parliament in London. It began on Wednesday after Easter and it granted the king a tax so wonderful that no one had even seen or heard of its like before. This is the way it was to be paid. . . .

[handwritten: poll tax]

Each earl of England	£4	
Each baron or knight	40s.	
Each squire of lesser estate	6s.	8d.
Each Justice of the Bench	100s.	
The Mayor of London	£4	
All merchants	13s.	4d or
	6s.	8d or
	3s.	4d or
Each archbishop	£6 13s.	4d.
Each married man for himself and his wife, if they do not belong to the people above mentioned and are over the age of 16 years, genuine beggars excepted, is to pay	4d.	

The court of Richard II

John Ball

Many people, however, evaded the tax and only £22 000 was gained from it. Two other poll taxes were approved in 1380 and 1381, and the last one charged one shilling per head and appointed tax collectors called Commissioners with very wide powers:

(5) You are to seize or arrest all those acting in opposition or rebellion to our tax: such men are to be held in our prisons. . . . Travel, with all possible speed, from village to village and make a list for the Treasury of all the people within every village.

Between 1370–81, landless labourers were few in number and could therefore demand high wages. The Statute of Labourers which was passed in 1351 fixed their wages at a low rate, however. As a result they became angry:

(6) Labourers that have no land and work with their hands deign no longer to dine on the stale vegetables of yesterday; penny-ale will not suit them now, nor bacon, but they demand fresh meat or fish. . . . Unless he be highly paid he will complain and curse the king and his justices for making a law that grieves the labourer.

The villein, the labourer who had strips in the open field and paid labour services to his lord, was also discontented. He began to object to the heavy labour services, as much as three days a week and extra at harvest time. In 1377 an Act of Parliament condemned villeins who:

(7) Refuse their customary services due to their lords and what is more draw together in great bands to menace the servants of their lords and to aid each other to force their lord with violence to agree to their demands.

The 1381 rebellion was helped further by a number of priests and wandering preachers, many of them thought to be followers of Wycliffe's Lollards. Perhaps the greatest was John Ball:

(8) For twenty years and more Ball had been preaching continually in different places such things as he knew were pleasing to the people, speaking ill of both churchmen and barons. . . . At last he was cut off from the Church and thrown into prison, and when he was released he preached a great sermon at Blackheath before 200 000 of the common people. He began the sermon:
    'When Adam delved and Eve span
    Who was then the gentleman?'
And continuing his sermon he tried to prove by the words of the proverb that all men were created equal by nature. If God had wanted to create some men lords and others serfs, surely he would have done it at the beginning of the world?

According to another chronicler, the real reason for the Peasants' Revolt was given by one of the leaders, Jack Straw, in a confession:

(9) And when we had assembled an enormous crowd of common people throughout the country, we would have murdered all those lords who resisted us. . . . Then we would have killed the king and driven out of the land all bishops and monks.

Questions and further work

1 Whom did the authors of Documents 1, 2 and 3 blame for the Peasants' Revolt?
2 What argument does the author of Document 3 use to support his opinion? Does the evidence in Document 4 support his opinion or not?
3 Imagine you are a village labourer in 1380. How would you feel when you heard about: (a) Document 4; (b) Document 5 and (c) Document 8?
4 What does Document 6 suggest about its author? Which words or phrases give you particular clues? If you had been a labourer what would you have felt about him?
5 Read through the whole chapter again. What did (a) the ordinary people and (b) their leaders contribute to the Peasants' Revolt?
6 How did the Black Death affect (a) the labourers; (b) the ordinary people and (c) the landowners?

17

The Hundred Years War

The reasons for the war

After the Norman Conquest the king of England owned land in France as well as in Britain. Henry II ruled Normandy, Anjou, Maine, Touraine, Aquitaine and Brittany (see chapter 7). This Angevin Empire, as it was called, was huge compared with the lands of the Capetian kings of France. They controlled a small area around Paris and, although they were recognised as kings of France, they were very weak and had no real power.

In the thirteenth century, however, the position changed. In 1204 King John lost Normandy, Anjou, Maine and Touraine to the invading

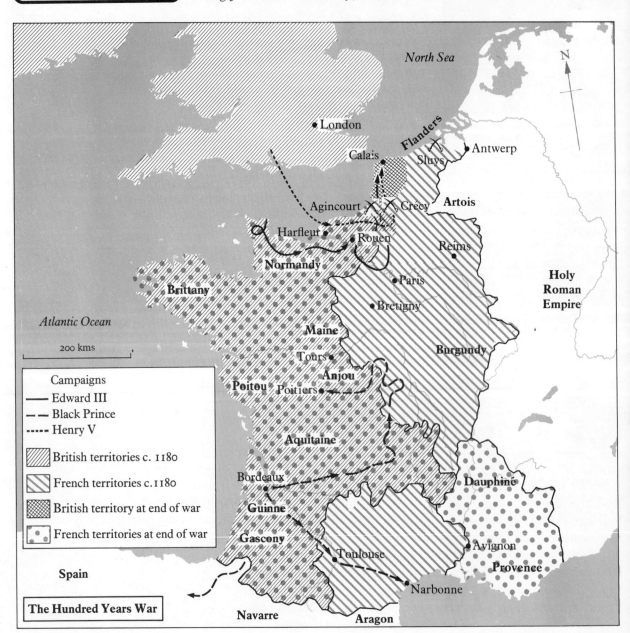

The Hundred Years War

Campaigns
— Edward III
– – Black Prince
···· Henry V

British territories c. 1180

French territories c. 1180

British territory at end of war

French territories at end of war

army of the clever French king, Philip Augustus. In addition John had to recognise Philip's nephew Arthur as duke of Brittany. In desperation John led two expeditions to try to recover Normandy but both failed miserably. Then his son, Henry III, also tried unsuccessfully to recover the lands and had to agree in 1258 to the Treaty of Paris. Henry kept a large part of Aquitaine but the French king, St Louis, was recognised in Normandy, Anjou, Maine and Touraine.

The merchants of England were not happy with this. They imported much French wine from Gascony into Southampton and Bristol, and the salt which they obtained from Poitou was vital to English fishermen and farmers. Both these areas were now under King Louis' control. Most important, however, was the export of raw wool to Flanders, another territory now coveted by the King of France. English merchants and sailors feared that their trade might be cut off by the French and they had reason to be gloomy. Edward I and Edward III spent their time in wars against Wales and Scotland rather than France. The accession of Edward III in 1327 brought to the throne a new and inexperienced ruler.

In the following year the last Capetian king of France, Charles IV, died. Who was to be the new king? Charles had no sons and all his brothers were dead. He did have a cousin, Philip, and a sister Isabella, who had married Edward II of England and was the mother of Edward III. Edward, therefore, had a better claim to the throne of France than Philip; but in 1328 he had only just become king of England and was too weak to prevent Philip taking the throne of France. Edward, however, always felt that he should be king of France. When in 1337 Philip declared that he was going to confiscate Guienne, Edward took the decision to invade France. This was partly to protect Guienne but also partly to assert his claim to the throne. The war which followed was to last on and off for over a hundred years.

1204	Philip Augustus captured Normandy, Anjou, Maine and Touraine
1258	Treaty of Paris
1328	Death of Charles IV and accession of Philip VI
1337	Philip VI confiscated Guienne

England's early success (1337–60)

By 1340 Edward's preparations were made and a convoy of over two hundred ships set sail across the Channel. As they approached the coast of Flanders near Sluys they saw a huge French fleet at anchor. The order to attack was given and the French fleet was destroyed. This was a vital victory for the English. England was now safe from invasion and English troops could be freely transported over to France.

Edward's method of attack was simple. He sent a number of able soldiers, each with a small army, to make a quick summer raid into an

The naval battle at Sluys

area of France. They burnt the vital harvest crops, raided buildings and manor houses and stole valuable gold plate. Before King Philip could mobilise his army against them, they had retired quickly to the coast.

Crécy

In 1346 Edward mounted his biggest invasion yet, sailing with over 12 000 archers and 2400 cavalry to Normandy with the intention of marching across northern France to capture Paris. This time the English met strong resistance from a French army probably three times as large. They were forced to flee towards Calais. The French caught up with them at Crécy and on 26 August the two armies met in open conflict.

The French army was larger than the English – one chronicler says eight times larger – but the English had time to choose a position on high ground, rest and have a meal before the battle. The French, on the other hand, were tired after their swift chase. This is how Froissart, one of the chief chroniclers of the war, describes the battle:

The French troops did not advance in any regular order: as soon as King Philip saw the English, he ordered his 15 000 Genoese crossbowmen to advance, but they were exhausted after a long march in full armour. . . . At this point a heavy rain fell and a great flight of crows hovered over the army making a great din. Then the rain cleared and the sun shone very brightly – but in the eyes of the French. The crossbowmen marched at the English, but as soon as they came within range, the English archers took one step forward and shot their arrows with such speed and force that they fell like a heavy snowstorm on the French. . . . At this the crossbowmen turned and retreated in panic.

The King saw their retreat and cried, 'Kill those scoundrels for they block our path in their cowardice.' But even the French knights were now being assailed by English arrows and they too fell back in confusion.

There were in the English army some Cornish and Welsh infantry who armed themselves with large knives. They advanced through the ranks of the French and fell upon their earls, barons and knights, killing many and annoying their own lord who had thus lost much ransom money.

What reasons can you find in Froissart's account for the English

The battle of Crécy. Describe the weapons of the two sides.

victory? Edward continued his march, took Calais and returned to England.

Edward's son played a major part in the English success in the first part of the war. Also called Edward, the Prince of Wales was nicknamed the Black Prince (probably because he and his retainers always wore black armour). Ten years after Crécy, he successfully used the same tactics again at the battle of Poitiers. He became a living legend: brave, daring, a brilliant general and yet honourable and trustworthy. When he captured King John of France on the battlefield at Poitiers, he treated him honourably, seated him in his own chair and served him with food which befitted the rank of a king. John was taken to England. In the peace terms of Bretigny in 1360 he was ransomed for three million gold crowns, a vast sum of money. By this treaty England also secured Aquitaine and the port of Calais, and had clearly won the first round of the war.

1346	Battle of Crécy
1356	Battle of Poitiers
1360	Peace of Bretigny

Henry V (1413–22)

The peace of Bretigny lasted just nine years and then for a while the French had the better of the war. The Black Prince and King Edward both died within a year, in 1376–7, and Edward's successor was the young Richard II. At the same time the French found a stronger king in Charles V (1364–80). He restored the French navy and fortified castles with paid mercenary soldiers under a new commander Bertrand du Guesclin. Unfortunately for the French, Charles died suddenly in 1380 and was succeeded by his young son Charles VI who suffered fits of madness. Peace was again made in 1396 between Richard II and Charles VI and Richard married Isabella, Charles's daughter.

It was in 1413 before England again had a king able to revive the war. Henry V was twenty-five when he came to the throne. He was slender but strongly built with dark hair, a straight nose and eyes which flashed angrily when he was crossed. On 11 August 1415 he set sail for France to recapture the territories which he claimed were his. With him he took 6000 picked archers and 2500 mounted knights. The town of Harfleur was captured by the middle of September.

Then a dramatic thing happened. Henry offered to fight single combat with the Dauphin, the French king's son. The winner was to take the French throne. The Dauphin refused as he knew that the English army had been weakened by plague and that his own army now numbered about 20 000. Henry tried to avoid battle by marching north to Calais, but the French moved quickly to bar his way.

Near the castle of Agincourt the two battle lines were drawn up. Henry was still not keen on a battle and he offered to surrender Harfleur

King Henry V

if his army could go freely to Calais. The Dauphin would only agree to this if Henry gave up his claim to be king of France. At this suggestion Henry knew that battle was the only solution.

Heralds from King Henry visit a French town

Agincourt

On the field, Henry sat astride his small grey horse with a jewelled crown on his helmet and his surcoat of leopards and lilies. Around him were his trusted English bowmen. At his order they marched forward to within 275 metres of the French. They fired their arrows at the dismounted French knights who were packed so close together that the arrows were bound to find their target. Many Frenchmen fell, and littering the field, made it difficult for those behind to come forward. Yet still they came on. The English yeomen put down their bows, took up swords and fought hand to hand. Many of the French were captured and the rest retreated.

But now the English line was confused and the third line of French cavalry was still unused, waiting for the call. At this point Henry heard that some French peasants were attacking his baggage train to the rear and that his crown and Great Seal had been stolen. He therefore gave the order to massacre all the French prisoners, a cruel but decisive action. When they heard of this the third line of French knights turned and fled. They never again obstructed his march to Calais and the coast.

Between 1417 and 1422 Henry was again in France and in 1420 he and Charles VI signed the Treaty of Troyes. Peace was made and Henry married Charles's daughter Catherine; Charles was to remain king of France but Henry was recognised as his heir and successor. He was now 'King of England and Heir to France'.

The final victory of France (1422–54)

Henry never became king of France, however, for he died in 1422 a few months before the mad Charles VI. Henry's baby son became Henry VI of England and the Duke of Bedford, an able soldier, tried to make him king of France, too. But the Dauphin, Charles VI's son, was regarded by most Frenchmen as king although he had not been crowned.

At first Bedford was successful and won most of the north of France. In 1428 he began to besiege Orléans hoping after this to march into the south. Orléans was surrounded by English troops when a young French girl arrived with a small company of knights.

She was Joan of Arc and she claimed to have been sent by God to relieve the siege. On reaching the city she rallied the French troops and the English were beaten. Joan then marched the young Dauphin to Rheims where French kings were traditionally crowned. Here he became king of France and, although Joan was captured and executed by the English in 1430, as Charles VII he finally drove the English from France. In 1435 he made peace with the Burgundians, who had formerly supported the English. The following year he captured Paris and in 1450 he defeated the enemy in the battle of Formigny. All that remained in English hands was the port of Calais.

An army builds a bridge to capture a town

1415	Battle of Agincourt
1420	Treaty of Troyes
1422	Deaths of Henry V and Charles VI
1429	Joan relieved Orléans
1430	Coronation of Charles VII at Rheims
1450	Battle of Formigny

A drawing of the battle of Agincourt. Again, notice the weapons.

The effects of the war

The war was fought intermittently for over a hundred years and it did considerable damage to the French countryside. English armies raided villages and plundered crops. Mercenary troops of both sides had to feed off the countryside as they fought. This account comes from a diary of the year 1422:

English troops were all over the region of Brie and were pillaging everywhere, so that it was impossible to till the soil or sow anywhere. Many were the complaints that came from farmers to the commanders, but they only mocked and laughed and their men behaved worse than before.

The war was not the only cause of poor harvests and famine, however. The plague and other factors also played a part. Even so, the war ruined part of the wine area of Burgundy; the population of France stopped growing and many villages, particularly in Gascony, were deserted.

How do we know?

The main account of the early parts of the war comes from the *Chronicles* of Jean Froissart. He was a French churchman, yet he regarded himself as essentially a writer. He wrote usually for a patron or employer and always tried to show his patron's side in the quarrel in a good light. (Between 1361 and 1366, for instance, he was secretary to Philippa, the queen of Edward III; between 1373 and 1382 he served the Duke of Brabant in Flanders). Since he always took care to revise and polish his writing, we can never be completely sure of its accuracy.

Using the evidence: Joan of Arc

What sort of a person was Joan of Arc? Was she, as the French thought a saint inspired by God and the angels to save France from the English? Or was she, as Englishmen suggested, a witch led by the Devil? Our knowledge of her comes largely from the evidence which was given at her trial. The first piece comes from a neighbouring farmer:

(1) As a child Joan was properly brought up in the Christian faith, so that all the local people loved her. . . . She spent her time in the fields, ploughing and

St Joan

guarding the animals, and she also did women's work like spinning and the rest. When she heard the bell toll for Mass while she was out in the fields, she came away to the church to hear Mass.

The next account came from a local farmworker who was a childhood playmate of Joan:

(2) I was brought up with Joan the Maid next door to her father's house. I know that she was good, simple, pious, fearing God and his saints; she often went of her own free will to church and to care for the sick and give to the poor. This I saw myself, for when I was a child myself I was sick and Joan came to comfort me.

We often find out about people from their comments about themselves. This is from the record of her trial:

(3) *Joan*: When I was thirteen years old I heard a voice from God to help me govern my conduct. It came about noon, in the summer time, in the garden of my father's house. The first time it came I was very fearful. . . . This voice told me twice or thrice a week that I must come to save France, to raise the siege which the English had laid to Orléans.
Question: How did you know the voice came from God?
Joan: I believed it quite quickly because I had the will to believe it.

Joan was eventually taken to the young King, who tested her: he hid behind a curtain before she entered the hall and gave his crown to one of his captains. When she came in, Joan immediately dismissed the captain and called for the King to come from behind the curtain.

The walls of the castle of Chinon

Fully armed herself, she then set off with a number of men-at-arms for Orléans. This was in April 1429 and at the gates of the city which was surrounded by English troops she gave this message to the English leaders:

(4) You, Duke of Bedford, who call yourself regent of the kingdom of France, give up to me, the Maid sent by God, the keys of all the cities which you have captured in France. . . . If you don't, then expect news of this Maid who will come to see you shortly to your great injury.

The French commanders outside Orléans had long been waiting for a favourable wind to send supplies up the river into the city. As soon as Joan arrived the wind changed and the supplies were sent. She also went into the city and began to rally the French soldiers:

(5) She had her armour put on by the lady of the house and her daughter; she told me to go and fetch her standard which was upstairs and I handed it to her through the window. She then raced towards the Burgundy Gate . . . where the English were preparing their defence. As soon as the French saw Joan they began to cheer and the bastion of St Loup was soon taken.

After Orléans was freed from the English Joan returned to the young King and marched him across northern France through the English armies to Rheims for his coronation. After the ceremony Joan:

(6) Embraced the King round his knees, cried joyous tears and said 'Gentle King, now is God's pleasure done. He willed that I raise the siege of Orléans and that I bring you to Rheims for your holy coronation. You are the true King now and God is on your side.' At this those who beheld the scene cried also.

After a number of other successes, Joan was captured by the Burgundians, sold to the English and handed over to the Church for trial. She stubbornly persisted that she was being guided by God but she was found guilty, condemned to death as a witch, and handed over to the English for execution. A Paris journal tells the story:

(7) She was bound to a stake on a scaffold of cement, on which a fire was built. She died quickly and all her clothes were burned away, then the fire was drawn back so that the people should not doubt that it was Joan. . . . Many people said that she was a true martyr and condemned the King of France for not rescuing her.

There was a story current after her death that it was not Joan but another woman who was placed on the stake. We shall never know for certain about this.

Questions and further work

1 (a) What did Joan's two neighbours say about her at her trial?
  (b) What did she say about herself at her trial?
  (c) What view of her character do we get from descriptions by other people at her trial?
2 Make a list of the points in the evidence which made people think she was a witch. (A witch is someone who acts on the instructions of the Devil.) Why do you think she was really executed? Give reasons for your answer.
3 Why did England finally lose the Hundred Years War? How did St Joan help the French (see Documents 4–6)?
4 Make a coloured timechart of the Hundred Years War. Beside each important date, make a drawing of the important event which happened at that date.
5 Imagine you were a newspaper reporter at the battle of Agincourt. Send back to England an account of the battle as you saw it. Include a headline and a plan of the battle as it appeared to you. You may also take comments from the participants to include in the account.

A sea-fight in the Channel

18

The later medieval Church

A parish problem

In Kent the parish of Kennington was dominated by a 'gangster' called Richard Rickard. He and his followers spent most of their time in alehouses. They slandered and often injured the people of the village. In 1411 the priest of the parish criticised Rickard in one of his sermons. As a result, the gang threatened to kill the priest and attack anyone who went to his church. On the following Sunday morning Rickard and his friends even sat by the church door to prevent the people from going to the services. Later, when services were permitted, they sat in the congregation and criticised the sermons in loud voices.

Kennington was clearly an unusual parish but the life of a parish priest in the later Middle Ages was often hard. It was difficult to persuade parishioners to go to church and some parishes had worse problems! Yet all over England there also was growing criticism of priests. Some priests still could not read, and others were often absent from their parishes or refused to do their duties.

A divided Church

By the later Middle Ages, many people were questioning the authority of the pope as head of the Catholic Church. The Church in England slowly drew apart from the Church in France and the Church in Spain. Many countries remained loyal to the Pope but by the sixteenth century a number, including England, cut themselves off from their ties with Rome. There were a number of reasons why this happened.

The Inquisition

The first of these was the Inquisition. In the thirteenth century Pope Gregory IX sent out a number of inquisitors, mostly Dominican friars, to all parts of Europe. Each one visited a town or a village and invited the inhabitants to criticise their neighbours and to point out those who did not believe in the Catholic Church. Spies were also installed in each town or village. Anyone accused was brought before the inquisitor and tortured to reveal his true beliefs. He was then convicted and punished.

Opposite Pope Gregory IX

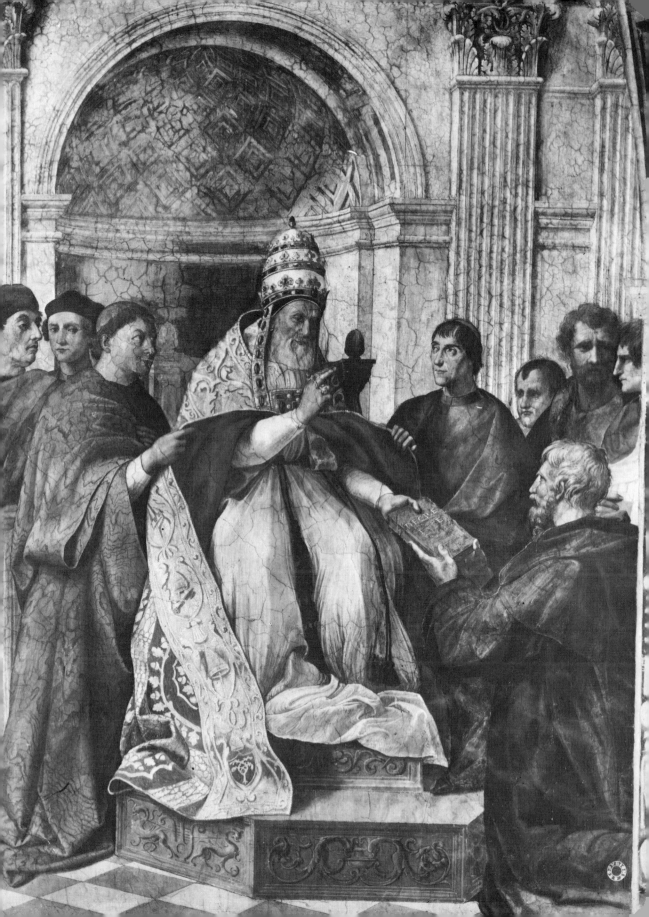

Methods of torture used by the Inquisition. Pictures like this were often drawn by the enemies of the Church.

Between 1308 and 1322 an inquisitor called Bernard Gui condemned 636 such heretics. Of these 321 were imprisoned, 107 burned, usually at the stake, and the rest were condemned to go on pilgrimages to Jerusalem or Spain. Only thirty-six managed to escape. The Inquisition, with its spies and torture, made the Church very unpopular in parts of Europe. But we must remember that in those days people really thought that criticism of the Church led to punishment in Hell. By this argument the inquisitors and torturers were helping their poor victims by enabling them to avoid the eternal fires and torments of Hell.

The Great Schism

In 1305 a new pope, Clement v, was elected. He was not an Italian. He was from Gascony in south-west France and he never actually went to Rome. Instead, he lived at Avignon, a city just outside the French border. He and his successors lived in Avignon until 1378. In that year, two popes were elected, one in Rome and one in Avignon and this became known as the 'Great Schism'.

Both the quarrel and the schism weakened the papacy, partly because popes were often concerned with great palaces and banquets rather than the religious life of Europe. One pope, John XXII, gave a banquet in 1324 when the guests ate 4012 loaves of bread, 55 sheep, 690 chickens, 270 rabbits, 3000 eggs, 2000 apples and much else besides.

John Huss at the stake

John Huss

While rival popes were quarrelling among themselves, several people argued for a different sort of church. One of these was a Bohemian preacher called John Huss. In 1408, he:

> began to preach and to reproach the people for their sinful lives. He then began to preach also against the sins of the priests, sparing neither the Pope on his throne nor the lowliest priest. He preached against their pride and their greed, against their wealth and their power.

Huss tried to show the people that they did not need the pope or priests to believe in God or to know how to pray. Many other people began to share his views.

In 1414, a Great Council of the Church was held. Bishops came from all over Christendom to Constance, in Switzerland, to do two things: firstly, to end the Great Schism and have one pope living in Rome; secondly to decide what to do about heretics like John Huss. The first aim was achieved in 1417 when Pope Martin V was elected in Rome as the sole Head of the Church. In its second aim, however, the Council was unsuccessful. John Huss was given a safe conduct to come to the Council to defend his beliefs. Then he was treacherously seized and in 1415 burned as a heretic. As a result he was looked on as a martyr all over Europe and still more people turned against the official Church.

Pope Clement V

The Church in England

If the Catholic Church in Europe was facing many difficulties, the Church in England had its problems too; the poverty and lack of education among the parish clergy was a distinct weakness. Perhaps one priest in every four was regularly absent from his parish church. The result was that there were no services for the people except those provided by a deputy, who was usually untrained and poorly paid.

Most priests, in addition, were badly educated: in 1530 Bishop Stokesley of London examined a number of curates to see how well educated they were. Out of the fifty-six men who were tested, twenty-two were declared illiterate and barred from continuing their work as priests; another six had to spend time in further study and come back for a second examination later. Out of these twenty-eight men, four had already gained the title Master of Arts from a University. So even apparently well-qualified clergy were sometimes too ignorant to continue their work.

Certain individual priests led bad lives and had to be punished in the bishops' courts. One 'was attracted to the wife of John Potter and she cannot be rid of him'. Other priests wore knives, swords, gold purses and other ornaments condemned by church law, including padded shoulders and long hair. Why do you think these were condemned? One writer even suggested that 'to meet a priest in those days was to behold a peacock that spreadeth his tail when he danceth before the hen'. Another priest played football in his shirt and usually finished his Sunday services before 8 a.m. to have the rest of the day free for games.

A priest gives the Eucharist to his congregation

In spite of these weaknesses, however, the Church did much good work. Parish priests collected a tithe, a tax of one-tenth on all farm produce. Part of the money went in alms to the poor. The priests also encouraged their parishioners to give money to poor people. One sermon described a lady who had two little dogs:

Every day she made for them dishes with sops of milk and often gave them meat. But there was once a friar who said to her that it was not well done that the dogs were fed and made so fat yet the poor people were so lean and famished with hunger.

Parish priests often tended the poor and sick, and advised parish guilds in their social work. They often also helped to produce miracle or mystery plays performed by the guilds.

John Wycliffe

Foremost among the critics of priests in England was John Wycliffe, a great scholar who lectured at Oxford University from 1372 to 1382. Wycliffe's home was in Lutterworth in Leicestershire and he could criticise the church freely because he was protected by the great nobleman John of Gaunt.

Partly as a result of his lectures at Oxford, Wycliffe quickly gained a large number of supporters who went round the country as 'poor preachers'. They were given the nickname of Lollards because their opponents said that they mumbled or babbled and did not speak clearly. In 1382 Wycliffe was tried at Oxford and his ideas were condemned. He died peacefully two years later but his ideas continued to spread throughout England until the sixteenth century.

Wycliffe criticised priests for two main reasons. Firstly, they were often wealthy, ignorant and unable to preach to the people. Secondly, they insisted that the Bible was read not in English but in Latin which ordinary people could not understand. Wycliffe argued that a man's belief in God should be based on the Bible alone and not on what he was told by a priest. People therefore must be able to read the Bible for themselves. Church leaders would not accept this, so in 1382 Wycliffe translated the Bible into English at Oxford. Unfortunately this translation followed the Latin order of words so closely that the English was very difficult to understand. However, by 1397 Wycliffe's followers had made a second translation in good clear English and it was this that circulated throughout the country. Over 200 copies still survive today.

Wycliffe's followers, the 'poor preachers', moved quickly throughout the country. Besides the University of Oxford, where many students and lecturers followed Wycliffe's ideas, the preachers found a willing audience in both town and countryside. A number of towns like London, Bristol and Coventry had large Lollard communities. It is more difficult to know the numbers in the countryside because men kept their views secret for fear of punishment. In 1414 Sir John Oldcastle led an unsuccessful revolt against the king and a number of his followers were executed. There was another riot in 1431, but by this time it was difficult to know precisely who the Lollards were.

John Wycliffe

How do we know?

By the later fifteenth century, the written evidence for historical events is considerable. Books were being written and printed. Chronicles, letters, diaries all give us more personal and individual information about people than we had for previous centuries. These were written not only by churchmen, but by laymen, too. Many copies of Wycliffe's Bible still survive together with accounts of trials of Lollards and the execution of Sir John Oldcastle and his followers. Yet, while we have so much evidence, it is difficult to use and we still know very little about the religious beliefs of the ordinary people.

Some badges carried by fifteenth-century pilgrims

1232	Pope Gregory IX started the Inquisition
1309	Pope Clement V moved to Avignon
1378	The Great Schism started
1382	Wycliffe's first translation of the Bible
1414	Council of Constance
1414	Sir John Oldcastle's revolt
1415	The burning of John Huss

Using the evidence: the Lollards

The leader of the Lollards, John Wycliffe, described his religious beliefs and criticised the Catholic Church in many books. Here are some extracts from his writings:

(1) Jesus Christ was a poor man from his birth to his death, shunning worldly riches. The Pope at Rome, by contrast, from the time of his birth until he dies, tries to be worldly rich. . . . Christ was the humblest of men, but it is said that the Pope is the most proud man on earth: he makes lords kiss his feet whereas Christ washed the feet of his apostles. . . .

Bishops and priests with all their deans and officials should not tax the poor people, for this is worse than common robbery. . . . It seems to true men that tenths or tithes should be divided between priests and other poor men who are feeble or lame or blind. . . .

Then there are the services of the Catholic Church: Matins, and Mass and evensong, commendation and Matins of our Lady. These are sung in trilled notes, by large choirs, to hinder men from understanding the meaning of what was sung. . . . Fools value these services more than the commandments of God and the study and teaching of Christ's Gospel.

Under Wycliffe's influence, the Lollard views spread rapidly. This account comes from Henry of Knighton, a Leicestershire monk, and was written about 1382:

(2) So the believers of these doctrines grew in number until they filled the whole kingdom. . . . A great number of people were foolishly deceived and drawn to their sect. They wore, for the most part, clothes of russet, showing outwardly the simplicity of their hearts, so they could begin their work of teaching and the sowing of their mad doctrine. . . . Over half the population of the country were won over to their sect, some from their hearts, others from shame or fear. They thought and preached that they alone were good men and worthy of God: those who observed the ancient and firm doctrine of the Catholic Church they declared to be sinners.

One of the most notorious of the Lollards was Sir John Oldcastle. He was condemned to death for his views in 1413, but he escaped from the Tower of London and in the following year led a revolt against the king. This account comes from a London chronicle:

(3) The same Sir John proposed to murder the King and his lords at Eltham on Twelfth Night in the evening. But the very same night the Mayor of London had word of it; so he took the aldermen and all the wards of the city and made great watch that night and captured John Burgate, a carpenter, and many others of the Lollard sect. Two days later the King and his lords came from Eltham to Westminster and took the field against Sir John Oldcastle's following and captured more than 8000 of his men. Twelve of them were immediately dragged from the Tower to Newgate and the next day another twenty-five were dragged. New gallows were made at St Giles for them and every one was hanged. Seven of them were burnt, gallows and all, and twenty-nine hung still on the gallows.

How were the Catholic Church and the government to deal with the Lollards? In 1401 an Act of Parliament was issued, 'On the Burning of Heretics':

(4) Many false persons do maliciously preach and teach these new doctrines against the holy Catholic Church; they make and write books, they wickedly instruct the people and stir them to rebellion. . . .

From henceforth, therefore, no one within the realm shall presume to preach openly without a licence from a bishop; no one shall make or write any book contrary to the Catholic faith, nor hold schools; anyone possessing books of such wicked doctrines shall deliver them to the local bishop within forty days. And if any persons be convicted of acting against this law, the severest penalty may be pressed against them; they shall be burnt before the people in a public place, so that their punishment shall strike fear into the hearts of others, so that no wicked doctrines may be tolerated.

Wycliffe's bones were dug up and burned forty-one years after his death. He was said to be a heretic.

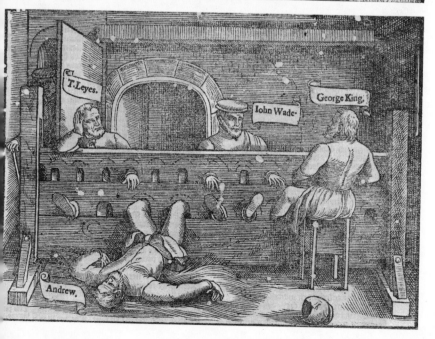

Methods of dealing with later Lollards

Anyone who was brought before a bishop, accused of being a Lollard, had to be examined or questioned. The following account comes from the evidence of William Thorpe who was first imprisoned in 1397 and later released. Ten years later he was examined again and asked about his teachers:

(5) Sir, Master John Wycliffe was considered by many to be the greatest thinker then living, a law-abiding and innocent man. Many people loved his learning and wrote it and followed his teaching in their lives.... Against this consider many Catholic pilgrims: examine any twenty of these and you shall not find three that know for certain a commandment of God. Many go on pilgrimages more for the health of their bodies than their souls, to have wealth, prosperity and enjoyment. Wherefore, sir, I have preached openly, and I propose to carry on preaching, saying that such people foolishly waste God's gifts in their sinful enjoyments.

Any man who continued to hold his beliefs after examination could be handed over to the royal courts to be burnt, as John Badby was burnt in 1410:

(6) A certain layman, a smith by trade, stubbornly refused to accept the teachings of the Catholic Church, so he was handed over to the king's justices to be punished. He was condemned and enclosed in a barrel in Smithfield and the Lord Prince Henry, who was present, came up to him and counselled and warned him to repent. The worthless wretch chose rather to be burnt than to give up his beliefs. The lid was then placed on the barrel and it was burnt and he groaned miserably amidst the burning. The Lord Prince was moved by these pitiful cries and ordered the materials of fire to be removed. He comforted the half-dead man and promised him life and threepence a day from the Treasury if he would repent, but the unhappy man, undoubtedly possessed by a devil, spurned the offer. Therefore the Lord Prince ordered the barrel to be enclosed again and the man was burnt to ashes.

The murder of the Lollard Richard Hunne

Questions and further work

1 What criticisms did Lollards make of the Catholic Church?
2 What did the author of Document 2 think of the Lollards? What evidence tells you?
3 What did the author of Document 5 think of (a) John Wycliffe, (b) Catholic pilgrims? What evidence tells you?
4 Make a list of the ways in which the Catholic Church tried to deal with the Lollards. Look carefully at Documents 4, 5 and 6. Why do you think the Church would not be able to stamp out the heresy completely?
5 Imagine you are a Lollard present at the burning of John Badby in 1410. Write a secret letter about it to the Lollard group in the next town.
6 Why were people becoming critical of the ordinary clergy? Make a list of the comments people made. Can you think of any reasons why the Church seemed to fail so badly at this time?

Index

Aachen 53, 55
Abderrahman 44, 45
Acre, kingdom of 114, 115, 117, 118
Aetius 16
Agincourt, battle of 206–7
Aidan, Saint 30
Ailred of Rievaulx 170, 171, 177
Aistulf, Lombard king 47
Alban, Saint 26–7
Albinus 32
Alcuin 52, 57, 63
Alemanni 28
Alfred the Great 19, 64, 65–6, 67, 148
Amphibalus 26, 27
Angevin Empire 202
Angevins in England 100–1
Angles 14, 18, 20, 27
Anglo-Saxon Chronicle 14, 15, 23, 63, 64, 65, 78
Anglo-Saxon learning 19
Anselm 88–90
Aquitaine 47, 202, 206
Arthur, king 20–3
Athelstan 66–7
Attila the Hun 16
Augustine, Saint 29, 32, 172
Avicenna 42

Badbury Rings 22
Badon, Mount 22
Baldwin 110, 111
Ball, John 199, 201
Barbarians, invasions of 14–18
Becket, Thomas 92, 184
    murder of 90–1, 93–5
Bede 19, 27
    writes history 32, 33, 34, 65
Belisarius, 36, 38
Benedict of Nursia, Saint 29, 171, 173
Benedictine Rule 171–3, 176
Beowulf 19, 27
Bernard, Saint 162, 170, 177
bishops and leaders 86
Bjarni 58–9, 68, 69, 70
Black Death 193–7
Black Monks 172
Bohemund 110
Boniface 32
bretwaldas 18
Buckingham, Duke of 12
Buda, king of Picts 30
Byzantines 107, 110, 115

Cadwallon, king 33
Caedmon 19
Calais 127, 128, 130, 204, 206–7 208
Cambridge University 184, 186
Canterbury 172
Capet, House of 55
Capetians 102, 103, 202, 203
Carloman 47
Carthusian monks 177
Catholic Church 214, 218, 220
Celts 14, 15, 23, 28, 30, 31
Charlemagne, king of the Franks 46–57, 61, 63, 65
    conquests 48–51
    crowned Roman Emperor 52
Charles II 'the Bald' of France 55
Charles III 'the Simple' of France 74
Charles IV of France 203
Charles V of France 206
Charles VI of France 206, 207, 208
Charles VII of France 208
Chaucer, Geoffrey 166, 169, 176
Chester mystery plays 156–9
Children's Crusade 106, 115
chivalry 162–4
Chosroes II, Persian emperor 38, 43
Christianity, spread of 26–30, 32
Church 214–19
    conflicts in 214–19
    and village life 143–4
Cistercian monks 125, 170–3, 176
Citeaux 172, 177
Clement V, pope 216
Clotilda, queen of Franks 28
Clovis, king of Franks 28
Cluniacs 172
Cluny, Abbot Hugh of 86
Cnut, king of England 67, 76
Colman 34, 35
Columba, Saint 29
    missionaries of 30
Constantinople 16, 36, 37, 40, 41, 43, 62, 107, 110, 111
Crécy 204–6
Crusades 106–9
    effects of 115–16
Cuthbert, Saint 30

Danegeld 67
Danelaw 64, 66
Danes 49, 62, 64–5
David, king of Scotland 170
Desiderius, king of Lombards 51
Domesday Book 79–81
Dominican friars 175, 214

education 180–9
Edward the Confessor 75
Edward I, of England 116, 192, 203
Edward II, of England 203
Edward III, of England 154, 162, 192, 203–4, 206, 210
Edward IV, of England 11, 19
Edward, Prince of Wales (Black Prince) 206
Edward, Prince of Wales, son of Edward IV 11, 12, 191

Edwin, king of Northumbria 18, 30
Eleanor, countess of Aquitaine 100–1
English overseas trade 128–31
Erik the Red 58, 59, 69
Ethelbald, king of Mercia 18
Ethelfrith of Northumbria, 18
Ethelred of Northumbria 18
Ethelred, 'the Unready' 68
Europe, countries of 102–3
    markets of 125, 127

fairs 125–7, 152
farming 137–40
Flagellants 196, 197
Flanders 125, 127, 203
Frederick I, Barbarossa, Emperor 103, 113, 114
Francis of Assisi, Saint 174–5
Franciscan order of friars 175–6
Franks 28, 36, 44
    under Charlemagne 46, 47–51, 55, 56
friars 174–6

Gaul 16, 45, 47
Geoffrey, count of Anjou 100
Germany 14, 48, 49
    invaders from 14, 22
Gildas 15, 23
Glastonbury 22
Goths 29, 36
Great Schism 216
Gregory I, the Great, pope 29
Gregory VII, pope 81, 86
Gregory IX, pope 214
guilds 148–9
Guthrum, king of East Anglia 64

Hansa towns 121–2
Hanseatic League 122, 128
Harold, king of Norway 74
Harold of Wessex 75, 76–7, 83, 84
Haroun al-Raschid, king of Persia 50
Hastings, battle of 76–7, 83
Hengist 14, 15
Henry IV, Emperor 81, 86
Henry I, of England 79, 100, 104
Henry II, of England 96, 98, 100–1, 102, 184, 202
    quarrels with Becket 93, 94
Henry III, of England 148, 203
Henry IV, of England 193
Henry V, of England 193, 196, 206, 207–8
Henry VI, of England 181, 193, 208
Henry I, of France 75
Henry Tudor 12
Heraclius 38, 40, 43
Hereward the Wake 79
Holy Land 106, 111–12, 162
Holy Roman Empire 103
Hospitallers 112, 162
houses 135–6, 147–8
Hundred Years War 103, 163, 166, 202–10
Hungarians 55
Huns 16, 17, 18, 49
Huss, John 217

Innocent III, pope 106, 175
Inquisition 214–15
Iona 29, 30, 62
Islam 40
Italy 36, 48, 51, 52, 81, 122–5, 171, 183, 194, 195

Jerusalem 38, 43, 81, 106, 107, 111–14, 115
Jesus Christ 27–8, 35
Jews 38, 82, 152–4
Joan of Arc 208, 210–12
John of Gaunt 198
John, king of England 101, 190, 202–3
John, king of France 206
John XXII, pope 216
juries 98, 100
Justin, Emperor 36, 37
Justinian, Emperor 36–8, 43
Jutes 14, 18, 20

King's Court 98
kings, duties of 97–100
knights, preparation and training 163
Koran 40

Law 98–100
Legnano, battle of 103
Leif, Erikson 59, 69–70
Leo III, pope 52
Leo IX, pope 86
Lincoln 146, 149, 152, 154
Lindisfarne 30, 62, 63
Lollards 201, 219–22
Lombards 29, 36, 47, 51
London 64, 146–7, 150, 153, 190, 197
Lothar 55
Louis IX of France 184, 203
Louis 'the German' 55
Louis 'the Pious' 55

Magna Carta 101, 190
Malik Shah, Moslem ruler 108
Malory, Sir Thomas 21
manor, life on 134–45
markets 150–2
Martel, Charles, king of the Franks 28
Martin V, pope 41, 45, 47, 108, 217
Mecca 39, 43
Medina 39, 43
Medina 39, 40, 43, 45
Meginard 86
Mercia 18, 30, 64, 78
Mohammed 38–41, 43
monks and friars 170–9
Monmouth, Geoffrey of 21
'More', 'Thomas' 11–12

Moslems 39, 40, 42, 44, 45, 55, 106, 107–8, 109, 111–13, 116, 187–8

Navigation Act (1382) 128
Nennius 20, 22
Nika riots 37–8
Ninian, Saint 29
Normandy, dukes of 74–5
Normans 74–5, 108, 110
Northumbria 14, 18, 30
Norwegians 62, 63
Nothelm 33
Notker the Stammerer 46, 47, 55, 56

Offa, king of Mercia 18–19, 50
Oldcastle, Sir John 219, 220
Ostrogoths 171
Oswald, king of Northumbria 18, 30, 33
Oswy, king of Northumbria 18, 30, 34, 35
Oxford 180, 183–4, 187, 219
    university 184, 218

Paris 183, 184, 185–6
Parliament 191–2
Patrick, Saint 29
Paul, Saint 28, 35
Paulinus 18, 30
peasants, life of 134–6
Peasants' Revolt (1381) 197–201
Pepin the Short, king of Franks 47, 48
Persian Empire 38, 40
Peter the Hermit 108–9
Peter, Saint 28, 35
Philip Augustus of France 101, 106, 113, 114, 117–18, 203, 204
Picts 14, 30
'Piepowder' court 152
Poitiers 41, 43, 44, 45, 47, 94, 108, 206

Redwald, king of East Anglia 25
Rheims 86, 208, 212
Richard I, the Lionheart, of England 101, 113–15, 165, 166
Richard II, of England 128, 192, 193, 197–9, 206
Richard III, of England 11–12, 191–2, 193
Richard, Prince, son of Edward IV, murder of 11–12, 191
Rievaulx monastery 170, 171–4, 177
Robert the Magnificent 75
Roland 49
Rolf the Ganger 74–5
Roman Empire 15–8, 36–8, 47
Romans 29, 30
Rome, under Charlemagne 52–3
royal household 96, 97–8

Saladin 113, 114
Saxons 18, 20, 21, 23, 27, 29, 48, 55, 56, 57
Scandinavia 61
schools 32, 52, 180, 182
Scots 14
sheriff, duties of 98
Slavs 49
Spain, Moslem 42
Stephen, pope 47
students 180–1, 185
Sutton Hoo ship burial 19, 20, 23–5
Syria 40

Tassilo, duke, of Bavaria 48
Templars 112, 162
Theodora, queen 36, 38
Thorvald 59
Tintagel 22
tournaments 165–6
towns 146–59
travel, difficulties of 120–1
Tyler, Wat 197–8
Tyrrel, Sir James 11–12

universities 183–6
Urban II, pope 88, 89, 108

Vandals 36
Venice 123, 124–5
Verdun, partition of 55
Vergil, Polydore 11
Verulamium 26
Vikings 32, 55, 58–72, 74, 75, 109
villeins 134, 135–40, 200–1
Vinland 59, 70
Visigoths 16
Vortigern, Celtic king 14

weapons and armour 165–6
Wessex 18, 64
Whitby meeting 30–1, 32, 34
White Monks 170, 177
Wilfrid 34, 35
William the Conqueror 75–8, 83, 84
    king of England 77
    sons of 79, 81
William, duke of Aquitaine 172
William II, Rufus, of England 86, 88–90, 103, 104
Willibrord 32
wool trade 125–31
Wycliffe John 199, 201, 218–20, 222

Zosimus 16